A TRUE STORY OF TWO WOMEN
UNITED IN THEIR SEARCH TO FIND
STRENGTH AND LOVE.

# Life of an Angel

# BRYNN JOHNSON
# CASSIE MILLER

On April 19th, 2013, precious Rowyn Leea Johnson was born to loving parents Cody and Brynn Johnson. She was born into a large family with deep roots in hometown Tenino. She received lots of love from her nanas, papas, aunties, uncles, and many cousins.

Rowyn spent her days trying to keep up with big brother Wyatt, being Mommy's helper, and Daddy's little shadow. Rowyn was a happy baby with a sweet disposition. She loved playing with other kids and would be caught red-handed giving boys hugs and kisses everywhere she went. Rowyn loved blowing a duck call. She would blow the call and laugh and laugh. She was always a lover, hugger, and would give you a pat on the back when you picked her up. Rowyn loved the outdoors. She would play in the sandbox with her brother, be in the garden with her mommy, or in the back with Daddy doing yard work. She was already learning how to ride her Power Wheels Quad, following Wyatt around the property of their home.

Rowyn had a big personality, always giggling and trying to make others laugh. She loved wrestling with her daddy. Her adventurous side would keep her parents on their toes. She was always scaling over baby gates, climbing on top of chairs and tables to start dancing. She loved music and would dance anywhere she went. Her favorite song was Meghan Trainor's "All About That Bass". Rowyn loved animals. She would chase her kitty Ruegar through the house to catch him and give him hugs. Rowyn was starting to talk and always said "hi" to every person she passed in a store. She loved to shop with Mommy and already had input on what she wanted to wear. She loved bright colors, and her favorite shoes were always Converse sneakers. Rowyn had bright blonde, wild curls that she always had a big bow in.

On September 16th, 2014, Rowyn Leea Johnson received her wings. Raise for Rowyn was started to keep precious angel Rowyn's memory alive and to give support to other families who suffer the loss of a child.

*Rowyn and her mother, Brynn Johnson*
*September 6, 2014*

*Rowyn Summer of 2014*

*Rowyn September 2014*

HE WILL *cover* YOU WITH HIS *feathers* AND UNDER
HIS WINGS YOU WILL FIND *refuge*.
PSALM 9:14

# Foreword

### BY Author

SHEY STAHL

It's hard for me to believe in something I can't see, as I'm sure there are a lot of other people in this world who feel the same way. It's the notion there's something bigger out there, and the faith to believe, but the mind is set in that it's not physically before me, therefore I can't believe in it.

There have been many times in my own personal life where I've wondered the meaning in life, and my purpose, as I'm sure most people have at some point.

One thing is certain for me now. People are brought into our lives for a reason, I do believe in that. It's not even that they're brought into your life, either. It's that they're placed in front of you for you to believe in.

On a beautiful September morning, as I sipped my usual iced coffee and stared off at the Olympic Mountains outside my office window, I came across a Facebook post made by a friend of mine that simply said: Hug your little ones tight.

I was in the middle of writing the eighth book in my *Racing on the Edge* series and a tad emotional given what I was writing about that morning; the death of a child.

As I read the post, I felt a tug to my heart, having just dropped my daughter off at pre-school that morning and the battle I faced there, having to pry her tiny hands from my leg while she cried and begged me to stay with her. Only a mother understands that struggle of separation, and hearing words like, "Hug your little ones tight," can sometimes make it worse.

*Did I hug her enough this morning?*
*Does she know Mommy loves her?*

While I wracked my brain about that, I focused more on the post made by my friend. She has two young boys and the message struck me as odd, so I messaged her, hoping everyone was okay.

My friend replied with the news that a good friend of hers had unknowingly ran over another friend's child in their driveway.

My heart dropped. I immediately felt for both the mother, and the friend.

I was in shock. Not only had I just been writing about something so eerily similar in my own novel, but I knew of Brynn, the mother of the child, from the salon where I had been getting my hair done. I'd never officially met her, but she was so bright, beautiful and full of life you couldn't help but notice her if you were in the salon at the same time.

I wasn't sure what I could do to help, but when a GoFundMe account was set up for the families, I donated what I could. It wasn't much at the time, but I wanted to help in any way I could.

It was months later—March, I think—and I was still working on my novel and preparing for my release in April, when I noticed Brynn was in the salon. I felt relieved that she was okay. If I had been her, I silently envisioned myself staying locked in my room for a good year if something so tragic had happened. Her strength was visible even then.

I sat there silently watching her, never wanting to say too much, so I didn't say anything.

I tried to put myself in her shoes and I could relate to the simplest of gestures, how even a 'sorry' could set someone off on an emotional breakdown that would take days to recover from.

Brynn seemed in good spirits that day, though her eyes marked a sadness not many of us would ever understand completely.

We chatted briefly about a book I was working on, and then I left. Cassie and Brynn had just begun blogging about their story and started Raise for Rowyn since the accident in September.

The entire drive home, I kept thinking they should write a book about their struggles and how far they had come. Just seeing her in the salon, living her life, going on, had been so inspirational to me that I couldn't help but wonder if it would help other grieving families do the same.

I felt so strongly about it that two weeks later, I messaged Brynn on Facebook and asked her if she'd ever considered writing a book, and if she had, I'd be glad to help her in any way I could.

She eagerly agreed and informed me yes, it was actually something she and Cassie had been discussing.

We met days later and talked about Rowyn and the accident, where I cried right along with her. I told her whatever she needed, I'd gladly help with. She gave me some incredible insight into the loss of a child, and the novel I had been working on.

In late May, I met with both Brynn and Cassie, where we had an outline to follow and they began telling their story. All of it. Even the parts you wouldn't think you would *want* to hear, they're in this book to give you an idea of what these beautiful, strong, caring and inspirational women went through, and found what they believed in to be true.

I wanted to help them any way I could and even envisioned the book down to the smallest details from the alternating chapters to the ending where it all came back to these two women and the journey they were placed on.

I've had the absolute pleasure in reading this book as it was being written and helping them craft their talent into writing a book.

While reading *Life of an Angel*, you will find pages upon pages of hurt, grieving, mourning, loss, and finally, healing through a belief and the will to continue.

When I look at Brynn and Cassie, I see two unbelievably beautiful who have souls that light up their eyes. Inspiring women who give me hope to continue on, even when you think of giving up on anything, from life to love, all of it. I have this phrase that inspired a series of mine, and I live by the words, much like these women do.

Give your heart, it's worth the pain.

I believe it is, and I believe Brynn and Cassie would feel the same.

I finally believe in something I *can* see.

Faith. To forgive, to love and to give the way they do.

You have to have faith that no matter what path you're on in life, you're on it for some reason, a greater cause than any of us can possibly imagine. Cassie and Brynn devoted themselves and their reason to something bigger. Something you couldn't necessarily see, but believed wholeheartedly in.

Brynn and Cassie were brought into my life for a reason, and I feel good knowing I helped them the best I could. They came into my life when I myself felt like I needed to make a difference and discover what it was I was doing.

When I first met them, they were only blogging their struggle. When I read the final novel they crafted, you have no idea the sense of pride I had knowing I helped them get their voice out there and maybe gave a grieving family hope, or another to donate.

I feel like there is a little bit of Rowyn everywhere, though I never met her.

To me, to be touched by a soul like hers gives me hope and faith in something I myself wasn't sure I believed in.

Shey Stahl

# Prologue

**BRYNN** | A MOMENT I'LL NEVER GET BACK

As Cassie's dark green Toyota Highlander started to pull forward, I continued to wave and smile to Wyatt.

I turned my head briefly back to the house to see what I thought would be Rowyn's little face looking at me through the window.

Only I didn't see her. I noticed the front door was swung open, and Rowyn was nowhere in sight.

Turning back to look at the car again for another wave at Wyatt, I saw Rowyn's little body slowly appearing from under the middle of Cassie's car.

In that split second, so many thoughts rushed through my mind.

*Oh, my God!*

# Chapter One

BRYNN

LOVE IN A SMALL TOWN

*"Be on your guard. Stand firm in faith. Be courageous. Be strong. Do everything in love."*
*1 Corinthians 16:13-14*

I was born in Centralia, Washington, on April 6, 1983. My early childhood was spent on my grandparents' farm in Rochester, Washington. My father wasn't in the picture much, but my mom always managed to provide being a single parent. I grew up not having much, but I would have never known we were broke. My mom and I lived with my auntie, and they shared a farm house down the road from my grandparents.

As a little girl, I loved to be outside playing in the meadows, being with the animals, and loved going to Grandpa and Grandma's house to help do farm chores. My grandpa Paul passed away when I was only four years old, but I still have many fond memories of riding his tractor through the fields and riding the lawn mower.

My mom had always told me growing up that my grandpa had such a soft spot for me and that we had a special bond. Even in adulthood, I have always felt this connection with him and continue to feel his presence when I need it the most. I would have never imagined how much I would one day still rely on my grandpa from the heavens up above.

Rochester, the town I grew up in, was a small farming community. We had one stoplight in town, a small corner market, and my high school graduating class was eighty-two students.

I loved growing up in a small town. I didn't come from a large family, but living in a close-knit community was where I found my support system. My love for the outdoors didn't change as I grew up. In high school, I spent my spare time riding quads or cruising up in the hills in my Jeep with my friends, sitting around bonfires, and going out to the gravel bar on the river. I always managed to get good grades but was in the principal's office quite often for rumors of me being at last night's party—which I usually was. I always seemed to get away with it, though. My mom tried her hardest to tame my wild ways, but my free spirit and independent nature made me a bit of a wild child.

The night I met my husband, I was just seventeen years old, and it was the fall of 2000. My best friend and I had made the fifteen-minute drive from the small town of Rochester to an even smaller town of Tenino. We walked into this old farmhouse, and I was instantly smitten with the most handsome boy I had ever seen. He had dark hair that was mostly covered up from his baseball hat, an olive-tan complexion, broad shoulders, and a smile I couldn't resist.

From the moment I laid eyes on him, I just knew we would be together. It was love at first sight. . . .or maybe lust. He was so handsome. That night, I actually told the friend I was with that I was going to be with him someday. I just knew it.

As I walked toward Cody, he looked up at me with his hazel eyes and long, thick lashes, and our souls connected. It was instant chemistry. I felt it for sure, and I hoped he did, too.

Cody was known for being quite the ladies' man back in his younger days, so my friend instantly rejected the idea. I was so offended she did so that we actually got into an argument about it.

"He's bad news, Brynn. You need to stay far away from him," she said, like she knew him.

I was upset that she would say that. "You don't even know him," I replied, annoyed.

It was just like me to want to prove her wrong, too. So, with a good amount of confidence on my part, I worked my way through the crowd of people nonchalantly, making my way toward him like a moth to a flame. Corny, I know, but so true. I couldn't help myself; I just had to get to know him.

He was there, head down, making drinks for some friends, and I walked up and asked him what he was making. Given it was fifteen years ago, I really can't remember the details of our conversation between the alcohol and butterflies, but I know my infatuation with him grew as we talked.

Somehow in the conversation, we both threw out there we were seeing other people. My gut told me someone as good-looking as him had to have a girlfriend. Guys like him are never single long. I was in a relationship, too, with someone I did care about, but this was an instant connection like I had never experienced before. We ended up exchanging numbers and went our separate ways for the evening.

AFTER THAT NIGHT, I still thought about Cody constantly. I felt bad for my boyfriend at the time because he was so nice, but clearly if I was daydreaming about some other guy than there was a problem. I knew I was going to have to break up with him soon.

Fate had a way of handling that for me. It seemed like after that night, I would run into Cody everywhere. I would always bump into him at different parties and even started seeing him at the local gas station. Every time we would see each other, our flirtation would get a little bolder, and he would get a little braver. He had told me he was single and wanted to take me out sometime. I had still been putting off the breakup but knew it was time.

I broke up with my boyfriend not long after that, and Cody and I started seeing each other a lot. We would go to mutual friends' houses together and have late-night bonfires. He had this big, jacked-up black Dodge Ram, and we would blast the music and cruise up in the hills all night long, laughing and singing. We both loved adventure and spur-of-the-moment decisions, so we would just hop in the truck and go wherever the road took us. Rodeos, motocross events, fishing trips, spending the weekends camping, and visiting any podunk bar I could sneak into.

Cody and I dated for nearly eight years before he proposed. People would always ask us what we were waiting for, that we should either break up or get married. Up until that point, we had a mutual hesitant feeling about getting married.

Having witnessed many divorces with our parents, and with friends already getting divorced, we weren't exactly rushing into it. We were so leery of making the permanent commitment to each other because we had never really witnessed a successful, healthy marriage that lasted for our parents.

When he finally popped the question, I knew it was right. It was Halloween of 2008, and we were home getting ready to go to our annual Halloween party at the local grange. Everybody in our small country town would be there. It was always a blast.

As I was frolicking through the house in my sexy Alice in Wonderland costume, covering the house with glitter and hairspray, I noticed how nervous and quiet Cody was. He wasn't acting very excited to go to this party. Not paying him any mind, I went prancing through the kitchen all wound-up, and he grabbed me by the waist. He picked me up and sat me on the kitchen counter. Staring into my eyes, he began confessing his heart.

"You are my best friend, the best thing that has ever happened to me, and I want to spend the rest of my life with you," he said, watching my reaction to his words.

I melted at his words because this was so intimate and special. He is a man of few words and not overly romantic, so to hear him opening up his heart melted me. He got down on his knee, pulled out the ring and popped open the box. I was crying, and so was he. I didn't even have the breath in my chest to say yes right away because I was too choked up, so I just nodded.

Cody picked me back up and I wrapped my legs around him. Then he spun me around in the kitchen, just hugging and cherishing the moment.

Pulling away, he looked in my eyes, waiting for my answer. "So, is that a yes?"

We both started laughing as I replied, "Of course. . . YES!"

Our celebration was short-lived when Cody ended up getting called into work that night. He was super bummed he couldn't go to the party.

I, on the other hand, was not about to pass up an opportunity to show off my new engagement ring. I called Cody's little brother Brett and asked him to be my date for the night.

After we arrived, I was so excited, buzzing around the room telling all of our friends and family about the proposal. It seemed like I was the only one who didn't already know it was coming. Cassie was also there that night. We even have a few buzzed-up girl group pictures floating around somewhere, celebrating the engagement. It was such a fun evening, a memory I will never forget.

Cody and I were engaged for over a year while preparing for our wedding. I was working full-time in the evenings as the food and beverage hiring manager for the Lucky Eagle Casino and also had decided to go back to cosmetology school during the day. Being gone six days a week and planning a wedding was a challenge.

Ultimately, after we got engaged, we knew we wanted children soon. That was my motivation to go back to school, so I could have a flexible schedule down the road to be home more with our future kids. I always knew we would have a boy. I could picture him long before we were ready to even start trying to have a child. We also decided before we tried getting pregnant that we would name our little boy Wyatt.

I always told Cody I knew we would have a boy and a girl. He would just laugh at me. He told me we wouldn't be so lucky to produce a girl in our family, coming from the man who has three brothers and one sister.

MARCH 19, 2010 WAS the day I married the man who had always had my heart. We decided from the beginning that we wanted the day to be intimate, with just our closest family and friends. We have an enormous family and many different groups of friends, so we knew the only way to achieve that was to have a destination wedding. After my months of planning and working extra hours to pay for it, the special day had finally arrived.

We were in the Riviera Maya, Mexico, and it was absolutely breathtaking. We chose to get married in a large gazebo sitting on top of the rocky pier over the ocean. The sounds of the waves lightly crashed below us. We were both so nervous we were trembling. The sun was starting to go down as I walked down the aisle lined with orange tiger lilies and exotic greenery toward him. As I approached him, we grasped hands and locked eyes.

*This is it,* I thought to myself, *the day we are committing the rest of our lives together.*

We kept our ceremony short and sweet, which we were glad about because we had a really hard time understanding our pastor. Between the language barrier and the crashing waves, it was comical trying to repeat the vows we were supposed to. After our ceremony, we had fireworks going off as the sun went down. I had finally married this boy everybody had warned me about. It was perfect, and I was still just as in love with the man that I finally got to call my husband. It was absolutely a magical evening.

# Chapter Two

CASSIE

## FIRST COMES LOVE THEN WHAT?

*"A baby will make love stronger, days shorter, nights longer,
bankroll smaller, home happier, clothes shabbier, the past
forgotten, and the future worth living for."*
*Author Unknown*

Life was so much easier when I was just nineteen years
old. I was in my sophomore year of college, attending school
at Central Washington University in Ellensburg. Living in
duplex housing among the other college kids, things could get
extremely wild and crazy along 19th street and Stonebrook.

It was the first Saturday night in early February, and I was
attending a birthday bash for one of my best friends and
neighbor at the time. One of her high school friends had made
the trek from Tenino to Ellensburg for the festivities. I do not
remember a lot about meeting my husband Aaron that night.
I was at a college party, but I do remember him wandering

into my apartment where I spanked him in a good game of foosball. We both had been dating people during that time, but Aaron, with his glowing blue eyes, brown hair and broad shoulders, claimed he had an eye on me from that point on. We shared small talk while listening to an album by the band, *Staind*, before wandering back to the street interweaving into house parties.

Several months later, he came to visit again with another friend, but that time it was summer. The busy streets, parties and people seemed to disappear in Ellensburg during the summer, but I was still in town working and taking summer classes. Aaron and I talked about my love for the town and school, and discussed my current class at the time, which was fly fishing.

Over the next two-and-a-half years, Aaron would make a few more visits to Ellensburg while I was there. However, other than chatting on the phone here and there, I didn't hear from him again until May of 2006.

At the time, I was living in Yakima where I had landed my first job. I was back in the Tri-Cities that weekend where my nephew was just being born. I had spent hours in the hospital with my brother and sister-in-law, waiting for his arrival. Like the proud aunt I was, I sent a text out to a few friends once he came into the world with all of his measurements. To my surprise, I got a text from Aaron soon after, congratulating me. Another friend was with him and had given him the news. I remember I thought it was really sweet and thoughtful of him to message me.

After that, I would hear from Aaron through text messaging now and again. I liked it when I did, but I never really thought he actually liked me or that we would end up dating. I unknowingly always assumed he would send me those messages when he had too much to drink. Never did I think there was intention behind them.

The following December, I had decided to head over to Tenino to celebrate the New Year.

After all, I had a couple of my best college friends living back in Tenino, and I knew Aaron was having a party. I had no idea going into that weekend that I would later be calling that man my husband.

We started the weekend off watching the UFC fights at friends' houses. We went to the Eagles club afterwards, where together we sang karaoke, "A Country Boy Can Survive".

The next morning was the day of his party, and I sent him a text that said:

*We can skin a buck, we can run a trot line and a country boy can survive.*

We arrived fashionably late to his party, of course, and in a change of plans, the group I was with wanted to go back to the Eagles. I didn't want to go, just wanted to hang out with Aaron more. So I asked him to come with us and he did. Aaron was my New Year's kiss and we ultimately spent the entire evening together, where he reminded me over and over again how much fun we would have if I lived there in Tenino.

When the weekend was over and I went back to Yakima, I was bummed. I felt like for the first time in maybe ever, I had actually connected with someone who saw all of who I was, and liked it. In that 'fantasizing little girl' way, I could see myself riding quads, hoofing through the woods, and his country boy life was so attractive to me. I couldn't believe I had never noticed it that much before. I really liked him, but we still lived three hours away from one another. To add an additional challenge, I had put in for a transfer with my work six months prior to this newfound relationship. I was weeks away from moving back to the Tri-Cities, which was an additional hour between us.

Despite the distance, it didn't stop us from talking on the phone. That was when I knew we had something. We started making plans to see one another, wanting to meet up again. It was then that something I never expected happened.

In a sudden twist of fate, my company changed hands at the Yakima office, and it then belonged under a new district manager who handled all of western Washington. The new manager came in my office determined to convince me not to leave his district. Instead, he explained what a better career choice it would be for me to move to western Washington, where he would put me in any office I chose.

It was quick, life-changing and risky, but I immediately wanted to talk to Aaron about it. I told him I felt crazy even considering doing it, but he told me I would be crazy not to think about it. I specifically told him I knew very few people in his area, and that I would be relying on him a lot.

He said, "Good."

I really wanted to do it, but the risk of us not working out would have been a big disappointment. I had to know he was all-in and serious about our relationship, and he was.

I took the offer and chose the Olympia branch. On March 6, 2007, my handsome Aaron moved me across the state, which placed me four hours from all of my closest family members.

I was raised in a small town called Benton City, where I was a twelve-year graduating senior in a class of eighty-two students. I was involved in everything from ASB, dance committees, sports and attending practically every party in our small town, unknowing to my parents. Or at least I thought they did not know. I grew up participating in rodeos, play days, team ropings, and easily could have taken on the term 'arena' rat as a kid. It seemed like growing up we were always with the horses at some sort of competition. My dad and brother took an annual hunting trip, and my hardworking parents, who started dating one another at age fourteen, just celebrated their thirty-sixth wedding anniversary this past October. Not only have I always been extremely close to my parents, but very close with my brother, his wife and my niece and nephew. Making that move was the hardest yet quickest decision I had to make for myself, but deep down, I knew it was the right one. My niece would call me on the phone upset asking, "Aunt Cas, why are you moving so far away?" It was heartbreaking to hear her tiny four-year-old's voice upset.

To give you an idea of how quickly Aaron and I moved along in our relationship, we had been dating just seven months when we made an offer on our first home together. Moving in to our new place was so exciting. We felt so grown up. We had a five-year plan to sell the house, build a shop to live in until our custom home could be built. These dreams were long gone we realized when the housing market took a hit. So for now our family of four resides in this 1310 sq ft home.

It was December 2010 when he called me and told me he had made a reservation for dinner for us at Anthony's, just a few days shy of Christmas. This country boy may be a bit romantic at times, but making a dinner reservation was not something he did ever. I was thinking and hoping that this was it. He was going to propose to me at dinner. I spoke to my mom several times before the dinner date, telling her I was really hoping that it was the plan, but I didn't want to get my hopes up. She certainly gave me no hints and played into the excitement with me. I later learned she had known the whole time, because Aaron had asked my dad for his permission.

I made sure my fingernails were freshly painted because I wanted the ring pictures to look good. I had wanted to marry Aaron for a while; after all, we had owned the house for over a year, had two dogs together, and yet despite those commitments, I wanted more. I was so excited about this night for weeks, but I couldn't help the overwhelming feeling of fatigue. It had been a long week with a house guest, I was doing some new training with my new job, and we had spent part of the weekend with Aaron's aunt and uncle in Portland. I was just completely worn out, but I was still so excited about the upcoming night.

To my disappointment, the dinner came and went. Nothing. He didn't propose. I had a glass of wine with dinner, which was so sweet I couldn't drink it, and he had a beer. We had normal conversations, and I kept thinking maybe he was going to do it after we ate, or maybe he would take me somewhere afterwards. It was all normal, and neither of those things happened.

As we were driving home, it sunk in that maybe he didn't want to marry me.

As we entered the house, neither one of us spoke. I kept thinking to myself, *why would he have taken me to a nice romantic dinner and not propose?*

Immediately, I put on my pajamas and started working on laundry. In the midst of doing that, I noticed how strange Aaron was acting.

At one point, he asked me to stop working on the laundry. His body was shaking when he squeezed me into a hug by our kitchen and said, "So, you wanna get married pretty bad someday, huh?"

I giggled a little, barely able to contain my excitement. "Yes."

As his entire shaking body sunk to the floor—on one knee—he pulled a ring out from the pocket of his jacket and asked, "Will you marry me?"

Of course, I said yes, and he slid the ring on my finger. We began texting and calling family and friends. I even posted it on Facebook. We were both on cloud nine. We were going to be getting married and we had decided long before this we wanted to do it in Tahoe.

Unfortunately, all that worrying whether he would propose or not made me tired. I accidentally fell asleep on the couch extremely early in our celebration. Not your most romantic engagement evening.

*The next morning*, I was making some caramel corn for Christmas gifts, and Aaron cooked us some breakfast. Neighbors were stopping by to congratulate us on our engagement, and I just didn't feel good.

I decided I should do some counting in my head, and as the numbers added up, something was wrong. I had a pregnancy test stashed in my cabinet from a long time before that. I didn't even tell Aaron I was taking it; I just wanted some piece of mind before I met my two girlfriends for a celebratory lunch. I was shocked as ever to see the positive sign pop up. I couldn't believe it. I was in pure shock. I yelled for Aaron to come to the bathroom, and he was just as surprised as I was. People kept reaching out about our engagement all morning, but I had many other things on my mind.

While in town trying to play the engagement cool, I bought five more pregnancy tests. I was so clueless that a person will rarely get a false positive; I had just known what I saw the girl in the movie *Knocked Up* do, so I did it, too. Of course, all five were positive, and we knew sure we were having a baby.

Aaron was very excited about the pregnancy news, but I have to admit I was in utter shock. During that time, I was reading the *Twilight* series, and I was on the fourth book, when Bella had a baby. I was waking up nights unable to sleep, crying because this was just not how I had planned this. Aaron woke up to find me in tears one night and he asked me,

"What are you so worried about? Do you think we are going to have a vampire baby?"

I was so comforted by his ability to calm me and be the strong one. It wasn't like I was too young, as I was twenty-five at that time, but it was hard to get used to the idea that there was a baby inside my tummy. A couple of days later, we were headed to eastern Washington to celebrate Christmas with my family. We read baby names aloud reciting what ones we liked and disliked. At one point, he reached over and grabbed my hand, saying, "I didn't think it was possible, but I feel so much closer to you now," I agreed.

We were having a baby, and I will never forget him saying that. We surprised my family when we got to town for Christmas with a little gift bag to open. Inside of the bag was a little baby suit that said, I love Grandma, and a little pair of baby cowboy boot slippers. Nobody was expecting that, but they were happy for us.

During my pregnancy, I started seeing a friend, Brynn, as my hairdresser because she had recently been licensed.

In fact, the first time she did my hair was at my house for me because she didn't even have a station yet. I had known her for a few years by that time, and when I heard she was getting her license to do hair, I really couldn't wait for her to be my hairdresser. She was beautiful, so I knew she would do her best to make me look good. She was also thoughtful and sweet, the type of person you can't help but feel comfortable around.

It didn't take long for little Easton Daniel to arrive on September 1, 2010. He was not an easy birth; I was induced at 41 ½ weeks and after delivering him, I suffered severe preeclampsia post-partum. In fact, I was very lucky I didn't have a seizure during his delivery. I spent extra days in the hospital under watch, but finally took our boy home. I was proud to have our little E-man, and more specifically knowing he would be a big brother someday.

WHILE I WAS PREGNANT with my son Easton, Brynn and her fiancé at the time, Cody, were planning their trip to Mexico to get married. It wasn't long after that when Brynn announced she was pregnant, and when the news spread she was having a boy, we had lots of hand-me-down clothes to pass along. I remember Aaron texting Cody excited that our two boys would one day be little hunting buddies.

It was June 17, 2012, nine months after Easton was born, when Aaron and I finally tied the knot on a beautiful boat on Lake Tahoe with our closest family and friends on board. We decided not to rush our wedding just because we had a wedding crasher coming. The day could not have been more perfect, and it was even more special to have our baby with us as we said our vows.

Shortly after being born, both Brynn's son, Wyatt, and my Easton started going to daycare at our friend Jen's house.

In no time at all, Brynn had baby number two brewing, as did I. Only she was having a girl this time, and I was having another stinky boy. Those clothes that had been passed to her for Wyatt were coming back to me in a big tote.

I remember getting my hair done at one point when Brynn was at the end of her pregnancy with Rowyn, and me at the beginning of mine with Logan. We were discussing how we were both going to be pregnant on our thirtieth birthdays, because we were born about a month apart ourselves.

Funny looking back that our pity party together was being pregnant over our 'dirty thirty' birthday. What a silly thing to even discuss. She was telling me about her appointment to get a 3D ultrasound, and I was hoping to get one done with my baby, too. Brynn never complained about her pregnancy with Rowyn; in fact, she told me she couldn't believe how easy and smooth it had all been. She looked and felt great the whole time. I was certainly jealous of that, but never in a negative way. I have always wanted the absolute best for Brynn and Cody. It is really quite amazing how much our lives have always paralleled one another's, yet I don't think we ever thought much of the similarities until this past year.

# Chapter Three

## BRYNN

### UNEXPECTED BLESSING

*"Every good and perfect gift is from above."*
*James 1:17*

It wasn't long after Cody and I married that we were expecting our first child. I found out on Halloween of 2010, coincidentally the same holiday that he proposed.

I was at work dressed up as a Jersey-licious Hairstylist—a popular reality show that was on at the time. Every Halloween, the salon girls would choose a theme to dress up as, so that was what we did.

Overly teased hair, too-tan spray tans, tons of gaudy jewelry, ridiculous makeup, long nails, and let's not forget to add that I was wearing hot pink and teal zebra print pants with a pair of patent pumps I could hardly walk in.

The salon girls had been planning this day for a while. We loved dressing up and having any excuse to go out for a good time after work.

Something was off with me that day, though. I didn't feel very good. We had been trying to get pregnant since our wedding in March, so I knew that was a possibility. I decided I better figure it out before a night out with the ladies.

So there I went, stumbling in my high heels down the sidewalk, like a baby fawn, to the local pharmacy to pick up a pregnancy test. Talk about embarrassing. First of all, even though I was married, it was still humiliating buying a pregnancy test, especially dressed like a provocative 80's queen. I made my purchase and was out of there as fast as I could be. I headed back to the salon the whole way, thinking, *there is no way it's going to be positive. . . but what if it is?*

I had butterflies in my stomach the whole walk back. I quickly rushed in the front doors of the salon, trying to be discreet with my pharmacy bag. I didn't want anyone to be suspicious.

I scurried to the bathroom to do the deed and waited there until I saw the positive result pop up. I was in shock. A happy shock, but I just couldn't believe it was real.

My secret was short-lived because I couldn't keep the excitement to myself. Plus, I knew the girls were going to think it was really odd that I was going to bail out on our night of fun. I ended up spilling the beans that evening before I left for the day. The salon girls were overjoyed, and they were ready to do some extra celebrating for me.

I went home that evening ready to share the news with Cody. Although I thought for sure he would pick up on the signs. I came home from work instead of going out with the girls, and I told him I was tired and wasn't feeling well that day.

I guess Cody was too distracted with shooting his bow to get the hint. I stayed outside with him for about twenty minutes, hoping he would get a clue, but he was oblivious. I went inside the house and changed out of my extremely uncomfortable clothes.

*I wonder when he's going to come in. I could be waiting all night before he decides to come in the house.*

Growing frustrated that he hadn't gotten the hint, I put on my comfy clothes and decided I was going to make this really clear for him. Taking the pregnancy test from my purse, I carried it outside, where I still struggled to get Cody's attention.

"Babe. . . babe. . . honey. . . "

Nothing. No reaction.

He was so focused on his damn bow he didn't even look at me.

Walking over, I grabbed his hand and placed the pregnancy test in his palm.

He looked at it almost confused for a minute, and then a big smile came across his handsome face. "Does this mean what I think it means?"

"YES," I said.

That got him to put the bow down as he wrapped his arms around me in the biggest hug.

With tears in our eyes, it was right then we realized our lives were changing from that moment on. We were going to be parents, a bond that would tie the two of us together forever.

We already knew we wanted a boy, and there wasn't ever a doubt that we wouldn't have one. We just kind of knew it was a boy.

Later on in the pregnancy, it was confirmed that it was, in fact, a boy. We were overjoyed and already had his name picked out, Wyatt Randall Johnson. We loved Wyatt because it was so strong and masculine. Randall was after his papa, Cody's dad.

During my pregnancy, we were in the process of buying our first home, crazy holiday schedules and struggling with everyday morning sickness. Cassie was actually preparing for her wedding during that time. I remember us discussing that she wanted a destination wedding. I attended part of her bachelorette party before her big day with my big belly. Our lives had become a whirlwind, but I loved every minute of it.

We moved into our new home in December 2010. I wanted everything to be ready for the baby to come, so Wyatt's room was one of our first projects. Cody was equally passionate about helping pick the décor, so I let him choose the paint colors. He chose a sage green with a dark brown wainscoting. I wanted to keep his room masculine and not over-the-top kid-themed, so I decided to stick with a rustic lodge feel. I picked plaid drapes and bedding for his crib. We hung little antlers on the wall and spelled out his name with wooden letters above his changing table. It was complete and ready for him to come long before he was.

Wyatt Randall Johnson was born on June 27, 2011. He was a week early according to my due date, but I felt more than ready to deliver. He was born at the Capital Medical Center in Olympia, weighed seven pounds, two ounces and was twenty-one inches long. A spindly little guy with long, lean legs, covered in this furry peach fuzz all over his body.

As I held my baby boy, I felt that unconditional love every parent before had told me about. Every parent knows what I'm talking about. It's a different kind of love than any other. It was so powerful that I couldn't hold in my emotion.

After Wyatt was placed on my chest, I just stared at him through my teary eyes. He was the most precious, beautiful little person I had ever laid eyes on, and he was *my* son.

From that day forward, our lives were forever changed, and it was the best feeling ever.

When it was time to leave the hospital, Cody and I were so anxious. We didn't know what we were doing.

*We get to just take the baby home now and take care of him all by ourselves?*

I remember how paranoid Cody was driving home from the hospital. I had Wyatt all snug as a bug in his car seat, and I sat in the backseat with him. Cody drove like a slowpoke grandpa on a Sunday drive all the way home.

When we arrived, we were greeted by our overly excited German Shorthair Pointer. This was the first baby she had ever seen. I had made Cody bring Wyatt's swaddle cloth home the day before, hoping she would adjust to Wyatt's smell. She was very cautious approaching the baby. I stayed very close and still had Wyatt in his car seat. She sniffed him and looked at me confused. Little did she know that little boy was going to be her best friend soon.

It didn't take long before Cody and I were in discussion of wanting another baby. Wyatt was growing up so fast, and we knew we wanted him to have a sibling. I loved the idea of having another little boy so they could grow up together playing sports and be in school at the same time.

A year later, we decided to start trying for another child; we didn't expect it wouldn't take long the second time. I got pregnant the first month of going off my birth control, so even though we were trying, it was still a surprise. We just didn't think it would happen so quickly. We were overjoyed and pleasantly surprised that my second pregnancy was much easier. I had hardly any morning sickness and felt great.

If I could have every pregnancy be guaranteed that easy, I would have a lot more kids.

When it was time to find out the sex of the baby, I wanted to do something different and special.

At my ultrasound appointment, I asked the tech to put the results in a sealed envelope so I wouldn't know the sex. We then took it to a cake decorator, who was the only person who knew the results.

It was right before Christmas, and we had a family trip planned to stay in a lodge and play in the snow. It was something our family had done the previous year, and we were making it our new tradition.

Knowing most of our family would be there, we decided to wait to find out ourselves and share that special moment with everyone. From my ultrasound to the trip, we had three days of waiting. It was the longest three days ever. We waited for everyone who was coming to arrive at the cabin that evening. We planned a big dinner, and I had brought a cake with me all the way from home, not knowing what the inside would be—pink or blue?

We all gathered around the kitchen table, gearing up for the reveal. Cody and I held the cake knife together, ready to cut in. We took one slice in and saw the pink cake crumble out as we pulled the knife through.

I was over the moon! I jumped up and down screaming, and Cody and I embraced.

"I can't believe it's a girl!" I said to everybody in the room.

Our whole family was crying, screaming, and laughing. We really didn't think we would have a girl. Once I knew she was, I was thrilled but a little terrified.

*What if she's a rebellious teenage hooligan like I was? What if she's a sassy back-talker like me?*

The thoughts of raising a girl seemed so intimidating, but I was tickled pink after seeing the inside of that cake.

Throughout my pregnancy, I had visions and dreams of my daughter. It was like I was getting a little glimpse of what she would look like. I envisioned her not as a newborn but toddler age, maybe around two years old. She had caramel-brown hair in curly ringlets, piercing bright blue eyes, long lashes, full lips, and an olive complexion like Cody's. She was beautiful.

Throughout my pregnancy, my bond was continuing to grow with this baby girl. We didn't have such an easy time agreeing on a girl's name. I had my heart set on Rowyn for most of my pregnancy. Cody and the guys in my family didn't really care for the name, but I didn't care. I was sticking to my guns. It just felt so right; I knew that was her name. It was a very strong feeling for me that she was Rowyn.

Rowyn Leea Johnson was born on April 19, 2013, at Saint Peter's Hospital in Olympia. My labor was a breeze. The only slight hiccup I had was spending most of my labor in a private waiting room of the hospital. They were so bombarded with deliveries that they had no open delivery rooms available. All I really cared about was that I got an epidural.

The staff took very good care of me, even though they were completely slammed. I got my epidural and everything was smooth sailing. I knew it was getting close to time, as I kept feeling the urge to push.

I had the nurses telling me to hold off just a bit longer. "Don't start pushing," they'd keep telling me.

They didn't have a room available yet, and they would still need to sanitize before I could go in there. I was holding back that feeling until they pushed me into a delivery room. It was within minutes that the doctor rushed to our room, ready to deliver Rowyn. She was welcomed to the world a short fifteen minutes later.

She was so calm and peaceful. I was almost concerned because she didn't even really cry. . . but she looked good. Nice color, nice and plump, healthy baby. The doctor placed her on my chest almost immediately after. You could feel her peaceful presence radiating off her.

I was so surprised that she didn't have the caramel-brown hair I had envisioned.

I kept saying to Cody, "I can't believe she has blonde hair!"

I was so certain the visions I had would be what she looked like. She didn't have the olive skin, either; she had my fair-skinned complexion. Though she wasn't what I expected, I thought she was absolutely perfect.

We were much more prepared and calm bringing Rowyn home. The second time around, we kind of felt like we knew what we were doing. Plus, we had everything ready for her nice and early, waiting for her arrival.

We decorated her room in a tiffany blue paint accented with a white border, like a bow around the middle of the room. My husband refinished an antique crib that was actually his as a baby and painted it coral. We spent so much time on all the details, from all the sparkle paint on the metal fixtures to the white-flowered crystal chandelier. I had her closet completely organized with all of her cute girly clothes, shoes, and accessories. Her room was my favorite in the whole house. So full of personality and color, just like our little girl would be.

After a very enjoyable three-month maternity leave, I knew it was time to get back to work. Fortunately, being a hairdresser, I had the flexibility to make my own schedule and only have to worry about finding childcare for one or two days per week. My kids as well as Cassie's were going to our good mutual friend's small in-home daycare.

Cassie's and my relationship continued to grow during this time. We saw each other pretty frequently and stayed in contact texting each other. She always would text me on the days she saw Rowyn at daycare, as she had this connection with her. She always complimented me on how cute she was dressed that day or what a good baby she was. We both loved having our kids growing up together in such a great environment. I felt so lucky to have found a good friend with children the same ages as mine.

We started talking about preschool for our older boys and decided we wanted to keep them in the same class growing up. Easton could technically be a grade above Wyatt, but we loved the idea of them starting preschool together and hopefully staying close friends all through their later school years. I thought Cassie's youngest son Logan was such a doll, too. He was always so happy, and he and Rowyn just loved each other. Ro would go up to him and give him kisses and huggies. We would laugh and say Logan was her boyfriend.

I was loving life and really felt like I had it made. I had the career I had always wanted, a healthy son and daughter with the flexibility to be home with them a lot, a hardworking and loving husband, and a great supportive family. I felt like my life was exactly where I wanted it to be.

CASSIE

SHE DREW ME IN

*"While we try to teach our children all about life, our children teach us what life is all about."* Author Unknown

The spring that Rowyn Leea Johnson was born, Brynn was extremely busy with weddings. She had bachelorette parties, bridal showers and weddings all in the upcoming months for some of her closest friends. I remember getting my hair done at the end of her pregnancy and thinking to myself, *How does she do it?* Because selfishly, that would be the last thing I would want to be doing at the end of a pregnancy.

Brynn is nothing like that. She is always putting others before herself. I received the *Breakfast at Tiffany's* baby shower invitation, but I wasn't able to make her shower. It seemed like Rowyn arrived shortly after, and I got the text April 19, 2013 she was born. Brynn took time away from hair for maternity leave, and when I was able to see her again for my hair appointment, she doted on her new baby Rowyn. I asked her how much she enjoyed her time off, and she said, "It's such a great time of year to be on maternity leave. I love being outside, planting flowers and just enjoying the kids and their time to the fullest."

I remember questioning her whether she thought she would have more babies, and she told me she was not opposed to having more kids if the pregnancy, delivery and demeanor of them would all be like Rowyn. At that point, I was also pregnant with my second child, and I already knew I did not intend to have any more because pregnancy was not something I enjoyed at all. Sweet little Brynn, of course, made it look like a cakewalk. I didn't know what I was having yet, but I would be lying if I wasn't hoping for a girl. Sitting in the chair in the salon that day and talking to Brynn, we were both hoping I would have a girl. Deep down, though, I always knew I was having a boy. I just felt like I saw myself being the mom of two boys.

The first time I saw Rowyn was at our daycare. Our friend Jen watched both of our boys, and was taking Rowyn for a few hours a couple days a week, too. Every time I went to pick up my son, she was always just sitting there looking around. Never crying, whining or even looking unhappy in any way. She was so perfect. Jen watched more than just our kids, and it was very easy to see that out of all the children there, teeny-tiny Rowyn may just have been the easiest of them all.

As time went by, I would usually see Brynn's kids when I was there picking up mine. Rarely did we cross paths, though, as we were on different schedules ourselves. Every time I saw

Rowyn, I couldn't help but notice she was just like her mother, with her blonde, curly hair, and always looking stylish as ever.

Our son Logan arrived on December 2, 2013. Rowyn was just eight months old. I kept Easton in daycare during my maternity leave, so we would see her and Wyatt there at times. By the time I went back to work at the end of February, Rowyn was really turning into a little toddler. She was getting mobile and her little personality was shining through.

I loved seeing her when I'd come to Jen's, but I usually only saw her a couple of days a week. Through the next few months, I'd see her with bright-colored bows in her white-blonde hair, Converse tennis shoes with bedazzled beads on them, little skirts with leggings and sometimes even overalls. I was just drawn to her, but I can't even explain why.

I would come home to my husband and tell him how cute Rowyn looked and what she was wearing. She would always come to the door, and eventually she would let me pick her up. I'd leave and find myself texting Brynn about how adorable she looked this day or that day. I always felt if I could have had a girl, I would have wanted her to be exactly like Rowyn. Everything about her was captivating. She had a little chin that is hard to explain, but it was pronounced. I would touch it when I saw her and just give it a little squeeze. Maybe because I have a pronounced chin myself it stood out to me, but for some reason, I just had to grab it while I spoke to her.

As the summer came to an end, we were preparing for preschool orientation and the boys' first day. At this same time, Jen decided to close up shop and move to working outside of the home. Brynn and I would text back and forth about what we were going to do, who we would trust with our babies, and if the other person had found an option of childcare. We were both coming up unlucky, even though we'd had the discussion many times before.

"What would we do if Jen ever quit us?"

Selfishly, we hoped to have her forever, but we both also knew it was in the cards someday. Someday was upon us.

Little did we know that, although this felt like such a trial for us as friends and parents, it wouldn't even hold a candle to what we were about to face together.

# Chapter Five

## BRYNN

### TRUST YOUR INSTINCTS

*"Trust the Holy Spirit when it dresses up like your intuition"*
*Bohemianbowmans.com/deeper family*

Life with a newborn and a two-year-old could get quite hectic, but it didn't take long before I got a routine down. Wyatt could be a handful when he wasn't the center of my attention, though, so it took some practice making everybody happy.

I breastfed Rowyn for eight months, and she slept in our room during that time to make feeding at night easier. She wasn't the best sleeper, but I didn't mind; she was the one and only person who could wake me up multiple times a night, and I would still have a smile on my face as soon as I saw her. The kids were complete opposites with their sleeping schedules, which actually worked out nicely. Rowyn would be my early bird, up at six AM, and we would spend a few hours together playing one on one before the Tasmanian devil named Wyatt woke up between eight and nine.

I used Rowyn's naptime to get some quality time in with Wyatt. She would go to bed an hour or so before he would, so we could have story time and give him the extra attention he needed, as well. I love being a mommy. It is the most satisfying and fulfilling job I have ever done. My favorite days with the kids are spent at our home in Tenino.

We have seven rural acres set back in a private setting, with a large yard for the kids to play in. In the summer, we spend every day outside that we can. We have blackberry bushes the kids and I would pick almost daily.

I would say, "Let's go pick our harvest for the day," and the kids would get so excited with their buckets, ready to go out and pick blackberries and raspberries. The kids love their fruit, so it would mostly be eaten before making it back into the house.

Rowyn would chase me around, saying, "Bite, bite, BITE!"

She was so funny. When I would give her a berry, she would make an exaggerated chomping sound with each bite.

We also have a raised garden bed we would tend to daily, as well. The kids would be 'big helpers', loading their buckets with whatever was ready to be picked. Most of the time, they would just play in the dirt, but all that mattered was that they were having a good time and spending quality time together.

Unfortunately, in the summer my husband worked a lot of hours and missed out on a lot of adventures the kids and I had. He missed the simple pleasures of staying home, as well as our vacation during Rowyn's last summer. Even though it was more challenging to take the kids on trips without Cody, we had many summer plans that I didn't want to give up just because I had to go alone.

In late July, I took a week-long trip over to eastern Washington. My mom and I met our side of the family in Sun Lakes for a few days of boating, camping, and family fun. From there, we went to Lake Chelan and met my in-laws for more boating and playing on the lakefront. This trip was filled with memories I will always cherish. During this vacation was also when I started getting very strong warning signals about Rowyn's safety.

Our drive to Sun Lakes was an exhausting trial. I finally realized why my daughter hated car rides. This being the longest car ride in her life, she threw up off and on the whole way there. My mom and I felt so bad for her. She was still so sweet about it, but the poor kid felt sick the entire drive over. She would only fuss for a short period of time before she would throw up and then have her happy little smile back on her face. Every time she threw up would be another thirty-minute 'pull over and clean up' session.

Wyatt, on the other hand, is an easy traveler. Thankfully, about halfway there they both fell asleep and slept the rest of the way. We rented a cabin at the lake and shared it with my cousin and her kids. It was far enough away from the water that we didn't have to worry too much about the kids escaping to the lake.

The park was set up like a little community, with cabins for rent, a tent camping area, RV parking, concession stands, and a souvenir and bait shop. After we got settled in and the car cleaned up, we took the kids down to the beach area.

Wyatt and Rowyn played in the sand with their toys and were happy babies.

Rowyn's curious nature would have her exploring before too long. She was such a fearless little girl that nothing intimidated her. She would get up, toddle over to the water and start quickly wading in without any hesitation. I got my workout chasing the kids around near the water. I was so nervous with whatever Rowyn was doing, but I didn't have that feeling with Wyatt.

There were times that he also would be wading in the water and I wouldn't be uptight about it at all. He is my cautious child and seemed to think things through before he acted—most of the time, anyway. I didn't have the worry about him that I did for Rowyn all the time.

Looking back on that trip, the fear actually consumed me. Another instance, we were sunbathing out in the yard area of the cabin, and I remember just being terrified Rowyn would dart out and get hit by a car. There was really no traffic and there were also speed limit signs of 5 mph all throughout the park, but I was consumed by that terrifying thought.

That night, after we put the kids to bed, my cousin wanted to have our ritual cocktails on the porch. I don't know how to explain the feelings I had, but I didn't even want to go out on the porch. I felt like that was too far away from Rowyn.

My mom was even in the cabin with the kids, yet still something told me not to get too far away. I kept going in the room and checking on the kids, seeing they were fine. I would be sitting on the couch in the living room, trying to relax and have some kid-free time with the girls, and I would be overcome with anxiousness.

*What if she gets suffocated in the blankets or falls off the bed? What if Wyatt is smothering her?*

I just couldn't relax and let loose. I was up every little while to check on the kids and finally just decided to crawl into bed with them.

The next day, we took the kids down to the concession stand for some ice cream. Rowyn's older cousins wanted to push her in the stroller. They were all taking turns pushing her along while we moms walked behind them. Even then, the thought was crossing my mind that they may push Rowyn out ahead of them and she may get struck by a car. I've overanalyzed just about every thought or feeling I had leading up to the accident, and I don't think it's a coincidence that almost all of my negative feelings or intuition involved her being hit by a car.

After our few days spent at Sun Lakes, we loaded up and headed to Lake Chelan. My father-in-law had his pontoon boat there, and we all rented a room at Campbell's Resort together. The resort was beautiful, with freshly updated outdoor areas and a sandy beach. It was fairly large equipped with a nice outdoor pool, hot tub, volleyball nets, BBQ grills, a giant shuffleboard table, and a clean beach. We spent most of our trip out on the boat or playing on the beach.

The trip was perfect, but once again, I was overcome by fear of something happening to my daughter. Not once did I have these fears about my son. I was so paranoid any time I was getting the kids out of the car, in a parking lot especially. Something in my mind kept telling me not to let go of Rowyn. I would basically juggle both kids on each hip, trying to safely get them from the car to a shopping cart or into the store.

I stopped at Safeway to pick up a few things for the room, and I had a very overcoming feeling of paranoia. Again, it was fear that she would get hit by a car in the parking lot. I was so bothered by the thoughts that had been overwhelming me that I confided in my mom about them.

After sharing my dreadful thoughts with her, she agreed, feeling the same thoughts. We both had the same instinctive fear surrounding her, but not Wyatt. Her feelings of worry had been getting stronger over the last few months and she was always fearful something was going to happen to Rowyn, as well.

Besides all my constant fear, we had a wonderful vacation. The weather was perfect, we enjoyed plenty of family time, good food, boating, swimming, and playing on the beach.

Rowyn even met her first boy crush. Our family was all down sitting on the beach, watching the kids play in the sand, and Rowyn was drawn to this blond-haired little boy. His hair was as white as hers, and they were about the same size. After talking to his parents, I learned that he and Rowyn were also the same age. They sat next to each other in the sand and gazed at one another. We joked and laughed about how much they liked each other. I was snapping pictures of the two when Rowyn leaned in for a kiss. It was the most precious moment, capturing her first kiss on camera.

I exchanged phone numbers with the boy's mother and sent her the priceless photos of our babies kissing on the beach.

After our fun-filled week, we made the trek back home and dealt with the same car sickness on the way back. Rowyn was such a good sport, even though she was miserable. I vowed I would not be taking her on any long road trips for a long time. I am ever so grateful that I did, though, or Rowyn would have never been able to experience as many firsts as she did on that vacation.

September 6, 2015 was my brother and sister-in-law's wedding day. We had been preparing for the big day for months. Rowyn was the flower girl, Wyatt the ring bearer, Cody a groomsman, and I was a bridesmaid. It was a perfect sunny Washington day, with just a light breeze. The girls spent the day on site at Cody's dad's home, primping and preparing together.

Rowyn, the baby of the bunch, stayed with all of us girls while we got ready. She walked around the room, exploring makeup bags and looking at all of the pretty girly things out on display. She was fascinated by the makeup brushes. Watching her Aunt Emily and me as I did her hair, she was so interested in what we were doing. Emily picked her up and sat her on her lap while we finished her hair. She didn't seem to mind the fog of hair spray and perfume; instead, she was just content to be hanging out with us.

After I finished styling Emily's hair, we finished putting on our makeup together. Rowyn gazed up at us so innocently but looked as though she wanted some makeup, too. I let her play with my makeup brushes and dabbed a little pink blush on her already-rosy cheeks. She smiled and giggled with enjoyment. My adventurous little girl certainly had a girly side, just like me. Girly enough to like all the makeup, hair, and shiny things, but she was not very happy about wearing her dress for the wedding. Her dress was a beautiful white, ruffled lace dress with a big satin bow off to the side along the bust line, topped with a denim vest. I put an oversized turquoise flowered headband on her, and she donned her tan cowgirl boots. She looked like a precious country angel.

With her fiery Aries attitude, she was starting to get impatient waiting to walk down the aisle. You wouldn't see her temper come out very often but when you did, you had better watch out. She squirmed out of her denim vest and was tugging up on her dress, starting to scream. I couldn't help but giggle at her because she looked so damn cute throwing her little tantrum.

It was almost time to head down the aisle, so I decided to nix the jean vest and we were just going to do the best we could. Walking down the aisle between Cody and me, she held both of our hands. The moment we went through the archway and she saw all the people watching her, she was in show mode. Her big, charismatic grin charmed all the guests as she walked down the aisle. She has had such a magnetic draw to her that everybody stared.

At the end of the aisle, Cody went to stand to the right with the boys and Rowyn and I went to the left to stand with the girls, just as rehearsed. It was short-lived, as Rowyn wanted to go stand with her daddy. She wiggled and squirmed until I released her to walk over to the boys.

Although it wasn't part of the plan, it was precious to see Cody reach out his hand to welcome her over. He picked her up and held her, whispering into her ear. Their connection and love was so evident.

I was so emotional that day, and it was definitely out of my usual character to be sobbing most of the time. I really couldn't pinpoint where all the emotions were coming from; it was just a mixture of so many things. It was so beautiful to see two people I love so dearly unifying their love.

As her dad walked her down the aisle, I couldn't help but feel a stab of pain not ever having a father to experience that with. I didn't have a father in my life to walk me down the aisle at my wedding. The only solid parent I've had was my mom, and she walked me down the aisle. I thought to myself how special that moment was between father and daughter. I then thought what a wonderful dad my husband is to our kids, and I know without a doubt I would never have to worry about Cody not being involved. I tried to picture Cody one day walking Rowyn down the aisle, and I just could not come up with an image of Rowyn as an adult.

I took pride knowing Cody and I would one day have our daughter's wedding to pay for and knew we would make it nothing less than amazing. Seeing how stunning Emily looked, I again tried to picture Rowyn one day in a gorgeous gown, arm and arm with her daddy as she walked down the aisle, but I could not come up with an image at all. My tears flowed as I was so overcome with my mixed emotions. It was such a happy day filled with feelings I just didn't understand.

On a sunny Sunday afternoon home with my family, I wanted to do something out of the ordinary. We always have Sunday family day, but I wanted to do something besides chores around the property followed by a BBQ.

"Honey, let's take the kids for an adventure," I said to Cody that afternoon.

I was really craving good quality time as a family. I threw out some ideas to Cody, but nothing seemed to appeal to him.

After being in discussion for way too long deciding what to do, we agreed on a family hike in the hills above our home. We packed a backpack stocked with diapers, wipes, snacks, water, and a plastic bag to pick wild blackberries.

Rowyn spent most of the hike on Cody's back in the pack, and Wyatt hiked along with us. She was so at ease, she fell asleep right away and rested her tiny face against her daddy's back. Her full lips were smashed slightly into a pucker position. I put her little baseball hat on to shield her face from the sun. The day was filled with special little moments for us and the kids.

About halfway through the hike, we stopped for a break in a shady part of the trail. I pulled Rowyn out of the pack and sat her down next to us to eat a snack and have a drink. The kids looked around us in magical wonder, fascinated by our surroundings, and found a hawk feather. Wyatt picked it up and showed his discovery to his sissy. We stuck the feather in Wyatt's hat and told him it was good luck. They both started picking the yellow dandelion weeds and showing them to Cody and me. Rowyn held hers up to her nose and sucked in a long, loud sniff. She then handed the dandelion to me, and I ever so gratefully accepted the weed. We decided to get back to the hike. Wyatt was getting tired and wanted Cody to carry him, so I took Rowyn in the pack and Cody carried Wyatt on his shoulders.

On the journey, we looked at different kinds of bugs and plants, stopping a few different places to pick blackberries. Cody showed us buck rub along some of the trees. Being knowledgeable in the outdoors, he explained what many different things were to us.

Though it was fun and interesting, the day seemed to be getting hotter and the kids and I were ready to head back toward home. We had a great adventure, but the kids were starting to get fussy and my back was starting to hurt from packing sissy. We had to walk a ways in the open field with the sun glaring down on us. Rowyn was starting to doze off to sleep again, and I reached back to feel her head. She was really hot.

That paranoia came instantly back to me. "Cody, we need to get the kids out of the sun. Rowyn is getting way too hot."

We were still a ways from home, and I had an uneasy feeling about Rowyn getting too hot. I took off her shoes and made sure the brim of her hat covered her face from the sun, as I felt like she was overheating. I picked up my pace to as fast as I could handle, even though I was already worn out. I just wanted to get the kids home. After what seemed like an eternity on the way home, we finally arrived back to the house. I got the kids in a cool bath and fed them dinner after. They were both wiped out from the heat and the day's adventures, so they were off to bed early that night. I never could have imagined that would be our last adventure together.

The next evening, I was preparing Wyatt's things for his third day of preschool. This was certainly a new routine for us all, and Wyatt was still very hesitant about going. The previous two days in school were pretty traumatic for both him and me. He would cry as we got ready for school and then would cling to my leg sobbing once we arrived. I would stay a few minutes with him, but his teacher assured me it was typical of many first-year kids and would be short-lived.

So after her reassurance, I would leave, becoming emotional myself. That evening, I was trying to prepare Wyatt ahead of time, talking about how nice his teacher was and how fun it must be to go to school with Cassie's son Easton. He still seemed very uninterested in going to school, however.

Cassie sent me a text message that evening offering to pick Wyatt up for school the next morning. I had been picking Easton and Wyatt up from school the last two school days and taking him back home. Cassie worked a full-time job and didn't have the ability to pick him up from school. I was more than happy to drive Easton home. It was a joy for me. He was always so polite and well-behaved, and I hoped his good manners would rub off on Wyatt some.

For some reason, I was hesitant on the idea of Cassie picking him up in the morning. I didn't know where the feeling of doubt came from. I fully trusted her, so that was not the issue, but I had an unsettling feeling in my gut about it. I didn't respond to her text right away; I needed to think the decision through. I couldn't understand why I was having a hard time with it, though. I knew Cassie felt like she wanted to contribute to the carpooling, too. She really wanted to help me out since I had been taking Easton home. Plus, I had shared with her how funny they were having their little boy conversations in the backseat. It was always hilarious. I would turn down the radio just to listen to what they would talk about: tractors, hunting some imaginary animal they made up.

I knew Cassie was excited to experience these little moments with our boys, as well. I could not pinpoint where my negative feelings were coming from, couldn't make sense of them. I also looked at it as I would get an extra hour to spend with Rowyn, and I could take my time getting ready for work.

Maybe Wyatt would be more excited to go to school if he got to ride with Easton. I decided I was being weird about it and texted Cassie back. I ignored that unsettling feeling in my gut and told her of course she could pick Wyatt up for school in the morning.

# Chapter Six

## CASSIE

### TRAGEDY, BUT NOT THE TRAGEDY

*"It's your road, and yours alone. Others may walk it with you, but no one can walk it for you."*
*Rumi*

My husband Aaron joined the Plumbers and Pipefitters Union back in early 2009. It was not an easy decision for him because he was comfortable working with a company doing new residential plumbing. However, he knew joining the union would open more doors of opportunity for him to do commercial work making more money.

At first, this job landed him at Fort Lewis, about forty minutes from our home. The transition was different for him, but he was learning a ton. When your husband works construction, the jobs always come to an end, as one way or another the project is finished. I knew this all too well, as my dad was a union electrician up until I was in college.

When Aaron's job finished, the company he was working for moved him to a new one in Bangor, on the naval base, which was farther away. The long commute would wear on him, but he never complained because he was happy to be working.

Before too long, he got in with a company called Plumbing Today Incorporated. This company would be the one to keep him working for the following five years. Each time a job would end, Aaron would be brought to their next one. The only problem with his company was that they were based out of Mt. Vernon, so all of the work was in Seattle or even further north.

He would spend a lot of hours a day sitting in traffic, driving his commute back and forth after his eight-hour workday to support our family. To give you an idea of the type of traffic I am talking about, it was sometimes three to four hours to get home from work on a Friday when his shift ended at two.

All that traveling wore on him as the years passed. He would be so tired that sometimes even holding a conversation would be hard for him.

I worked full-time myself, so we were definitely a busy working family.

It was the end of July 2014 when Aaron was at work on a community college in Bellevue. He was working on the ground level at the time, and there was a crew of ironworkers working fifty feet up from him. He saw something out of the corner of his eye and heard a loud crash, like something had just fallen to the ground.

Immediately, the apprentice working beside him yelled, "He's down, he's down!"

Aaron ran to see what it was and unfortunately, he ran up on a very tragic accident.

It was an ironworker who had just fallen that fifty feet face-down, and Aaron was the first person to get to him.

He yelled, "Buddy, are you okay?" There was no answer, and very soon there was a puddle of red seeping out from under him.

Knowing the man wasn't okay, Aaron yelled, "Call 911!" and stayed with the guy. He also helped usher the paramedics in.

Sadly, with a fall like that, it was as anyone could have expected: he was killed instantly. The young man was very close to our age, had a wife and young kids.

Aaron didn't know him, just his name and that he had family. Shaken up, he called me as he was sitting in Bellevue answering questions with paramedics and labor and industries. Helicopters for news stations were flying above, and he was worried I would hear of it and panic.

"It's bad. It was so bad," he said, sounding extremely shook up as he began to describe to me what had happened. "I was working alongside the apprentice when we started hearing this loud crashing sound. I thought it was just material that had dropped from above, so I didn't pay much attention, but then the apprentice said 'Holy shit, he's down, he's down!'"

Aaron sounded scared as he described what happened to me. It was probably the first time in all the years I had known him that he sounded terrified of anything.

Given the circumstances of the accident, Aaron had to wait for more questioning but then said as soon as they would let him leave, he would call me.

He drove straight to my work and I met him in the parking lot. He just kept saying, "It was bad, it was so bad."

The next day, the job was shut down. When I came home from work that day, he was just different. He was distant, quiet, and seemed to be doing a lot of thinking in his head. I could tell this was bigger than I had realized at the time.

The job opened back up two days after the accident, but there was grief support prior to the start of the shift. Aaron made the long drive to Bellevue that morning, and to my surprise he called me just as I was getting to work to tell me it was too hard. He left and was driving home.

It scared me to hear him sound like that. In all the years I've known my husband, he didn't just miss work. In fact, he is such a devoted employee he usually arrives twenty minutes early to start his day. And in those last eight years, I could count on one hand how many days he has called out sick.

I immediately called my father-in-law to get some advice. I didn't know if he had heard about this accident, or if he knew Aaron was witness to it. He had actually heard of it, but had no idea his son was at the scene.

I was crying as I spoke to him, saying, "I have never seen him like this. I'm not sure what to do."

"Wow. Oh, man, I had no idea. I'll call him and talk to him, but Aaron is a tough guy and he will be okay," he said, trying to assure me everything would be fine.

At that point, Aaron had no intention of ever returning to the job in Bellevue; he knew he couldn't face it. I think that was what scared me, because if it was so bad that he couldn't return to work, how could I possibly begin to understand what was going on inside of his head to help him?

Aaron's company gave him some time off, but offered to get him back to work when he was ready at a different job-site. I got in touch with the employee assistance program and referred Aaron to them. He called and met with a counselor to discuss what was going on. I work with psychiatrists as well, so I tracked down my favorite one to ask her what I could do for him or what to expect from him. She said it was still so acute that he needed to take some time to process what had happened still. He was in shock, she told me, and in a couple of weeks he might start to seem normal again.

Aaron described it as hardly being able to look at our own kids without crying, getting scary flashbacks of the scene in his head at times. And although he was able to sleep at night, there was certainly alcohol assisting with that.

After a couple of days, Aaron had a revelation. One he had been turning around in his head for a couple of years, but this basically validated the decision. It was time to part ways with his loyal company, be closer to home for more time with his children. He had always said he felt like such a dirt ball after he would get home because he had no energy to spend the time with them he wanted. I completely supported him with his decision, and reassured him that neither our kids nor I ever saw him that way.

The following Monday, Aaron called the big boss of his company and offered his two-week notice. They were extremely sorry to hear the news, but they understood, as not many people could keep sane with that commute daily. They paid him for two weeks, but he never had to return.

In the midst of all of this, we were in the search for daycare providers. I thought it was just a blessing in disguise because Aaron could stay home awhile. When he was called out to work for a more local union shop, we could worry about childcare then.

Not so fast. Two weeks after Aaron's accident, he got a call out for a job in Woodland, which is an hour south of our home, for a local company. He knew he had to take it, and he was excited about it.

I wasn't sure it had been enough time; in fact, I wanted him to stay home for a while and rest. I couldn't change his mind, though, and pretty soon he was back to work and I was back on the daycare hunt.

It was at the point where I was texting Brynn every day to see if she had found anything. Only neither of us was having much luck.

One afternoon, I was on a walk with friend and coworker, Amy. I was describing this difficult situation I was in with daycare hunting again. She thought I was crazy that I'd rather have my husband unemployed than have to search for daycare at that time. But honestly, my baby was only eight months old, and I knew it wouldn't be easy to find someone I trusted to care for him. Just dropping him off at a daycare facility seemed scary.

"I just need to find some young college kid who wants to take classes at night or online and have weekends off to come be my nanny," I told her, thinking that was exactly what I needed.

"I wonder if my niece would be interested in doing that," she contemplated.

I said to her, "You have had this niece this whole time and you have been holding out on me?" "I have never thought about it," she replied.

Within a couple of days, her sweet niece was at our house to meet our little family, and we gave her the job.

By that point, it was August, so she would be starting September. Everything was going great for us. Aaron was a few weeks out from his accident and finally coming back to normal, liking his new job and his new commute. Easton and Logan got along great with their new nanny, Easton was starting preschool, and I had a good job working as a supervisor for the state. I had only been in the position five and a half months, but I was finally getting more comfortable with my new role.

It had been such a good couple of years. I would be lying if I said I hadn't thought on a few different occasions that things had been good for so long that something bad was probably going to happen soon.

# Chapter Seven

## BRYNN

### OUR LAST MORNING TOGETHER

*"Enjoy the little things in life, because one day you will look back, and realize they were the big things."*

*Author unknown*

"Mom. . . Mom. . . Mom. . . Mooooooooooom!" I heard my daughter yelling from her crib.

Rolling over, I grabbed my phone to check the time. It was 5:32 in the morning.

"Ugh!" I grunted, knowing it was time for me to crawl out of bed.

Rowyn continued to call for me until I made my way down the hall and peered into her room. When she spotted me, her eyes sparkled with excitement and she smiled from ear to ear.

I giggled at her because she was so happy that it instantly rubbed off on me the second I saw her.

You couldn't look at her smiling face and ever be irritated, even at 5:30 in the morning.

Picking her up from her crib, I snuggled her, enjoying my morning loves from her. She wrapped her chubby little arms around my neck to give me a hug, followed by her patting my back as I carried her to the changing table.

As I changed her diaper, we talked and giggled. I decided to keep her dressed in her turquoise and white polka dot pajamas. It was a brisk morning, and we had plenty of time before we needed to get ready for the day.

I loved our mornings. This was another typical early one spent together as Wyatt snoozed away.

Carrying Rowyn downstairs to the living room, I set her down with some toys to play with.

I scuffed over to the Keurig to pour myself a cup of coffee. Rowyn was already full of energy, running around the living room and giggling.

*Oh, I would give anything to wake up with that much energy.*

After I had my cup of coffee brewed, I joined Rowyn in the living room. I sat down cross-legged on the floor and set my coffee up on the table.

Since this was a common routine for us, Rowyn pointed at my cup. "HOT," she said then ran toward me and leaped into my arms.

She loved to wrestle on the floor, a habit she learned from her big brother. So she tackled me and we giggled some more and rolled around on the floor. I knew I had an hour or so before I needed to get Wyatt up for his third day of preschool. I wanted to do something special for him.

Grabbing my phone, I checked my Pinterest boards for easy breakfast recipes. I scanned through different recipes, showing sissy the pictures.

Cinnamon apple croissants was the one I showed her.

"Mmmmmmm mmmmm," Rowyn said when she saw the picture.

So cinnamon apple croissants it was.

Rowyn continued to play in the living room with her toys as I went to the kitchen to start preparing breakfast. She would occasionally run into the kitchen to see what I was doing.

Once I put the croissants in the oven, I turned on the oven light so we could watch them rise. I set the oven timer and went back to the living room, sitting cross-legged to finish my coffee and play with Rowyn some more.

The morning wasn't anything out of the ordinary for me, but I seemed more observant and aware than usual. I was taking all the little details in. I wasn't in the typical morning rush to get everyone ready, and I truly got to enjoy every little moment that morning I had with her.

At 7:15, it was time for Wyatt to get up and get ready for school. He was not my happy early-riser.

In fact, he was the complete opposite. He wasn't very happy when his sister climbed into his bed to tackle him with morning love.

"It's time to wake up, buddy," I announced, like it was something so exciting. "You get to go to school today."

He grumbled and groaned as he flung his comforter over his head. "I DON'T want to go to school!" he shouted.

*Oh, boy, somebody woke up on the wrong side of the bed today.*

"Mommy and sissy made you a special breakfast this morning. Would you like to come downstairs and eat before we get ready?"

He ignored me.

I continued coaxing him for what seemed like forever until I finally decided to just pull his covers off.

"Come on, I'll carry you," I said, picking him up out of bed, knowing I was going to have to give him some extra attention that morning.

I couldn't trust Rowyn yet to get down the stairs by herself, although she sneakily did it all the time. So I picked her up, as well. I had forty-pound Wyatt on one hip and twenty-three pound Rowyn on the other and carefully carried them downstairs.

*No wonder my back always hurts.*

Coming down the stairs the house smelled of baked cinnamon and apples. I sat Wyatt down at the kitchen table and placed Rowyn in her high chair. I served Wyatt his still-warm apple croissant first and cut Rowyn's up into small pieces for her.

All my excitement was short-lived when neither one of them would eat it. Wyatt picked a few bites at his but refused to eat it, and Rowyn would have nothing to do with hers.

I, on the other hand, thought they were delicious and ate a couple of them.

In my frustration, I gave Wyatt the lecture that there are many kids all over the world who don't have food to fill their bellies and they would be so grateful to have this breakfast.

I checked the clock again and couldn't believe what time it was. The morning rush was on, and I needed to get Wyatt ready for school. Cassie was planning on being over at 8:10, and we didn't have much more time to waste arguing over eating breakfast.

I dressed Wyatt in the outfit I had picked out the night before. "This is your third day of preschool, Wyatt. Are you excited to see Easton and Mrs. Riggles?" I asked.

"NO! I am not going to school!" he yelled back at me.

*Lord, help me with this child.*

The morning battle continued as I dressed him. Wyatt, my strong-headed willful child, doesn't do anything he doesn't want to without putting up a fight.

His father and I are the same way, so I can't be too surprised.

Finally, after struggling to get him dressed, his teeth brushed and hair combed, we all went back downstairs to wait for Cassie to arrive.

"She should be here any time, so watch out the window for her." I checked my phone again for time, and Cassie had texted me saying she was running a few minutes behind.

I debated to myself if I should put a little makeup on before Cassie arrived or comb my hair because my appearance was embarrassing.

*She's a mom, too, and I doubt she's going to judge me by what I look like right now.*

I decided to keep the white bathrobe on, un-brushed hair and not a stitch of makeup on.

A few minutes later, I saw Cassie coming down our long driveway. The kids were running through the house playing and screaming at that point.

"Wyatt, Easton and Cassie are here!" I yelled for him to hear me over his and his sister's crazy-loud play session.

"NO, no, no, I don't want to go to school," he said. And then he started to cry. The real cry. Tears were streaming down his cheeks. He really was nervous about going to school.

The previous two days had been challenging as well, but I knew I needed to be consistent. I knew once I got him adjusted to the new routine it would be good for him. He really needed to develop the social skills with other children.

Cassie pulled in the roundabout gravel driveway in her green Toyota Highlander.

"Okay, Wyatt, it's time to go." I grabbed his backpack that was sitting on the bench by the front door.

Wyatt was still crying. Reaching for his hand, I opened the front door. "Come on. You're going to school, and it's going to be really fun today."

Sis was standing next to us as I was trying to convince Wyatt that school was going to be really fun. I practically had to drag him out the door. Shutting the door behind us, I left Rowyn inside. She peered out the side window next to the front door and watched us as we walked down the front steps of the house toward Cassie's car.

Wyatt's fit didn't stop. As we made it to Cassie, I realized I forgot his booster seat in my car.

"I'm going to run and grab his booster!" I yelled to Cassie as she was getting out of the car. "I'll be right back."

I left Wyatt at the end of the sidewalk while I ran to the other side of the house to get his booster out of my car. In a hurry, since we were already running behind, I grabbed it quickly and ran back to load up Wyatt in Cassie's car.

When I came back around the house, Wyatt was no longer where I left him. He had run back into the house to hide.

In my frustration, I looked at Cassie. "I'm so sorry!"

She was laughing and didn't seem to be stressed about the situation. I quickly walked back to the house, still holding the booster seat. Opening the front door, where both kids were standing still watching us out the window, I grabbed Wyatt by the hand again.

He dropped to the floor, screaming and crying.

*Oh, my God, seriously? Is this really happening right now?*

Rowyn was looking at me innocently, like 'what in the heck is going on right now?'

Kneeling, I picked Wyatt up off the floor, knowing there was no way I was going to get him through the front door on his own.

I had Wyatt on one hip while still holding the booster seat in the other arm and then saw his backpack sitting on the floor. I was about to my limit of staying calm. I knelt down with both arms already full and barely managed to grab his backpack, too.

*Okay, here we go again. . .*

I could barely open the door my hands were so full, but after I managed to do so, I walked through and hooked it with my leg, swinging the door to close behind me.

As I juggled everything down the steps and sidewalk toward Cassie's car, she was still smiling at me.

I felt embarrassed that I was holding her up from getting the kids to school in time. She probably thought I just got up since I was still in my bathrobe.

I apologized again as I threw Wyatt's booster seat in the car. "It never fails. No matter what time I get up, it always seemed to be a struggle to get everyone ready," I told her.

Cassie laughed and agreed, still calm as could be. She didn't seem to be bothered by my screaming son one bit. I buckled Wyatt into his seat and sat his backpack on the floor of the car.

His tears were not letting up and his fit had basically turned into begging at that point. I was reassuring Wyatt again that he was going to have a great day at school.

Easton tried to comfort Wyatt also, as he was actually really excited to go to school. Cassie got back into the car, and we were making small-talk.

"Are you sure you want to deal with taking him to school? I honestly don't mind at all taking him. I don't expect you to listen to him crying the whole way."

"He'll calm down as soon as we get on the road," she said, reassuring me it wasn't a big deal.

I knew she was right, so I gave Wyatt a kiss and told him I loved him. I shut the car door and stood at the end of the sidewalk as they were leaving.

I waved and smiled as they started to pull away.

# Chapter Eight

CASSIE

THIRD DAY OF
PRESCHOOL

*"From the outside looking in, you don't understand it. From the inside looking out, you can't explain it."*
Author Unknown

As the old saying goes, "Everything happens for a reason," and by that point, I was really starting to believe that. We were finally on a better track with Aaron's new job and smaller commute, the nanny we had hired and my new flexible working hours.

On the morning of September 16, 2014, things felt quite ordinary. Still getting into our new routine with the preschool schedule, I was now working 9-5:30 on the Tuesdays and Thursdays we had school. This allowed me to be able to take Easton to school every day so I didn't have to instill my nineteen-year-old nanny with the duties of driving the boys around.

I wasn't comfortable with her driving them yet; these are my babies. Brynn had offered to bring Easton home from school on Tuesdays and Thursdays for me, but at my hair appointment just four days before the accident, I had learned she now had an after-school sitter.

That hair appointment in a sense is very important to this story. We had some good conversations about our families, how short life is, and how quickly our kids were growing. I shared with Brynn how I wanted to plan a surprise trip to Disney and tell Aaron and the kids at the same time. She shared with me that she had just done that exact thing, and surprised her family with a trip to Mexico.

Before I left the appointment, I said, "This week will be the last one you have to bring him home on Thursdays for me, and I will get my nanny to do it after that."

She didn't mind, of course, so her response was, "Oh, honey, it's no big deal, seriously."

I knew, however, that there was no need for her to drive to pick up my son from school when she did not have to even pick her own up.

The evening before the accident, September 15, 2014, I texted Brynn at about 8:00PM. I asked her if she would like me to pick up Wyatt in the morning and take him to school. She didn't need me to, and I later learned she didn't even really want me to, but she knew I wanted to help out with the carpooling, so she said sure. I told her I would be at her house around 8:10 Tuesday morning.

That morning, I was getting ready and shuffling around with this thin linen paisley scarf. It was coming into fall, and it was one scarf I had that was thin enough for September but looked like fall.

I remember putting it on and wondering to myself, "Why am I even wearing this?"

The scarf was something I had only worn one time before and it was to a funeral. For some reason, I sort of did the shrug-your-shoulders thing in the mirror and went with it.

Logan wasn't even awake that morning when we left. The nanny arrived and Easton and I were headed over to Wyatt's to pick him up.

When we got in the car, before even leaving the driveway, I turned around and looked at Easton. He was so cute and starting to look more like a little boy every day. "Aren't you so excited? This is your third day of preschool!"

He grinned really big because he totally was. His beaming blue eyes and blond hair really brought out the bright orange and blue in his button-up collared shirt. He looked so handsome that day, with gel in his hair and his little jeans.

He liked to repeat the plan to me. "Yes, and then we're gonna go pick up Wyatt and then Wyatt's mom is gonna bring me home after."

"That's exactly right," I told him. He made sure to call his papa on the way to Wyatt's because it was his birthday. He was able to leave a message for him.

AS WE MADE THE drive to Brynn's, we were listening to the local country music station. Easton could get quite animated when he was singing in the backseat.

At one point, I looked in the rearview and he was just singing his little heart out. I'll never forget it because the song that was playing was Lee Brice's, "I Don't Dance". Easton was singing "I don't care" instead of dance because he thought those were the words.

The image of this beautiful blond-haired, blue-eyed four-year-old had just made my whole day. It was a very proud mommy moment for me.

The sun was shining so I had my sunglasses on, and we were on the five-to-seven minute cruise to Brynn's house. I am not that person who was late often. It is important to me that I be on time, so getting the boys to school on time was something I tried really hard to make happen.

Everything was normal when we arrived at Brynn's house around 8:10.

I got out of my car to see Brynn carrying Wyatt out of the front door and down the porch steps. She was wearing a white robe, which made me happy because it meant she was relaxing and not rushing around. I had gotten out of my car to greet them.

Wyatt, however, was not happy. He was crying, saying, "I don't want to go."

Brynn, trying to calm him down, said, "Wy, honey you have to go. It's your third day of school."

Brynn had to walk around to the back of the garage to get Wyatt's car seat from her car. As soon as she slipped out of sight, he raced back up the front porch steps and into the house, shutting the door behind him. Brynn's dog, Kimber, was right at my feet with her blanket and balls. She is always looking for someone to toss her a ball.

When Brynn made her way back over, she asked, "Did he just go back inside?"

"Yes," I told her.

With a little sigh of irritation, she walked back up the front steps to go inside to get him. That time, when she came carrying him out, the front door was left open.

Within seconds, little blonde curls, footie pajamas and a smile that could melt your heart appeared. She slowly made her way down the front steps backwards, and once to the concrete walkway, she started running toward us.

"Hi, Rowyn," I said as she grinned from ear to ear.

We were standing at the passenger side of the car, but about three feet from the back end. She was still on the little concrete walkway beside the solar light. I reached down and gave her little tiny chin a squeeze. It was my favorite.

Brynn appeared to be at her wits end by that point, but Wyatt was in the car and buckled to go.

"You know," I said, looking at her, "I'll just go and he'll be fine."

"Are you sure?" she asked, the anxiety of the morning evident on her face.

"Yeah, I'm sure. We'll be fine once we start going." I walked to the driver's seat of my car, leaving Rowyn back at that spot on the concrete walkway.

Brynn and Cody have a pull-around driveway, so I knew I wouldn't be backing up or anything. Climbing into the car, I looked at Brynn through the backseat passenger window.

"We'll be fine," I said to her again.

She waved to me and the boys. I looked at the clock as I put the car in drive. 8:18.

In this split second, the thought going through my mind was whether we were going to make it school on time.

*Yay, success for the third day of school.*

Little did I know that I was about to play a role in Rowyn's destiny, or that I was about to play out a role in my own.

# Chapter Nine

## BRYNN |

### THE ACCIDENT

*"He will wipe every tear from their eyes. There will be no more
death or mourning or crying or pain, for the old order of
things has passed away."*
*Revelation 21:4*

As Cassie's Toyota Highlander started to pull forward, I
continued to wave and smile to Wyatt.

I turned my head briefly back to the house to see what I
thought would be Rowyn's little face looking at me through
the window.

Only I didn't see her. I noticed the front door was swung
open and Rowyn was nowhere in sight.

Turning back to look at the car again for another wave at
Wyatt, I saw Rowyn's little body slowly appearing from under
the middle of Cassie's car.

In that split second, so many thoughts rushed through my mind.

*Oh, my God!*

I was confused. *What the hell is she doing there?*

She was face-down in the gravel, her turquoise and white polka dot jammies standing out lying in the driveway.

I ran over as fast as I could and scooped her up. I knew right away she was not breathing and started screaming.

I have no idea what I was screaming at that point, but I know shock instantly set in.

As I held her screaming, I looked up and saw Cassie's eyes in the rearview mirror.

In that second of our eyes meeting in the mirror, I knew she saw the panic on my face.

She immediately stopped the car and flung open the door as fast as she could. "What happened?" she screamed. "OH, MY GOD, OH, MY GOD, call 911!"

Rowyn's body remained limp in my arms, unresponsive and peaceful.

Having no concept of time while any of this played out, I wasn't sure what to do, but Cassie grabbed her cell phone from the car and dialed 911.

I stared down at Rowyn's face, which looked fairly normal.

*She can't possibly be dead! She looks fine! How the hell did this happen!?*

Her body and head did not feel normal to me. I was clinging to her little twenty-three pound body with my hand supporting her head. Everything just felt soft.

*Had her body been crushed completely?*

I could tell by the way she felt in my arms that it was not good.

Cassie was on the phone with 911 and ran over to me. "Give her to me!" she yelled.

Cassie then grabbed her body, laid her on the grass in my front yard and started on CPR.

I didn't know what to do. I stayed with them for a few moments, unable to process anything.

It was then, as Cassie performed CPR, that I saw Rowyn's mouth pooling with blood.

"Oh, my God!" I cried, my hands clasped over my mouth in horror at the sight of my baby bleeding.

I ran into the house in a panic and called 911, even though Cassie already had. It felt like the longest sentence I had ever heard when they answered the call.

I just started screaming, "MY DAUGHTER IS DEAD! I need help now! Like now! Hurry up, I need a miracle!"

As the dispatcher was trying to calm me down and asking me the standard questions, I couldn't even focus on what she was saying. I was pacing in circles through my kitchen and ran back outside.

Kneeling down by Cassie, I watched her perform CPR and looked at Rowyn. Her face was swelling and blood was everywhere.

Unable to control myself, I started screaming again. "OH, MY GOD! LORD, PLEASE HELP ME! SAVE MY BABY GIRL! I NEED A MIRACLE!"

I was again circling in the yard, still on the phone screaming, crying, begging and pleading with God and the dispatcher to give me a miracle.

I was getting pissed that it was taking so long. "Where the HELL are they?! I need help now!"

"They are on their way, ma'am. Try to remain calm. I assure you that they are on their way. Is there anybody else in the home with you?" she asked.

I remembered then that my husband was upstairs sleeping. "My husband," I replied.

He had worked graveyard and only gotten home a few hours prior.

I ran back into the house as fast as I could and into my bedroom upstairs. "CODY, CODY, CODY!" I screeched.

He quickly sat up in bed and stared at me with a horrified look on his face. "WHAT?! Whose blood is that?!" he shouted.

I paused, staring at him with a blank face, not knowing what to say.

I didn't even know I had blood on me.

I looked down and my white bathrobe was drenched with blood. My hair was stained red, as well.

"Rowyn. . . Rowyn. . . I need you, Cody!" I begged of him. "You need to save her!"

He gazed at me in disbelief, nothing but shock registering on his face. "What the FUCK do you mean ROWYN?" He flew out of bed in just his underwear and ran past me. "Where is she?"

"She's outside. . . You *need* to do CPR. You *have* to save her, Cody!"

I was desperate. Some little hope in me thought he could fix her.

He could save her.

He *had* to save her.

I rushed down the stairs after him and we both ran outside together. I watched him staring at our daughter in disbelief.

Having snapped into action, he pointed at Rowyn and screamed at Cassie, "Who the FUCK is this?!"

I had never seen my husband panic. He was always so calm and under control, and to have him freaking out in that moment made me realize the significance behind our situation.

*Holy shit, this is real!*

"WHERE THE HELL IS HELP?!" I shouted into the phone.

The dispatcher calmly assured me that help was on the way again.

I have no idea how long it actually took for them to get to us, but it felt like an eternity.

A roller coaster of emotions took over me. I was in denial and disbelief one minute with hope that she was going to be okay, and then filled with rage the next, crying and cussing at God. One emotion crashing into the next, never letting up.

Staring down at my daughter, I just knew deep down she wasn't going to come out of it. That didn't stop me from praying and clinging on to any little bit of hope.

I continued to beg God for a miracle.

In the next moment, I saw a Sheriff SUV speeding down the driveway with lights on.

*Thank God! Somebody is here!*

He hurtled into the driveway and ran over to Rowyn to take over CPR.

Cassie and I fell to the ground a few feet away from Rowyn in the front yard. As more firetrucks, police officers, and ambulances flew down the driveway, we huddled together in the grass sitting cross-legged.

I don't know what we talked about. We were both in shock.

Cassie twitched and rocking back and forth. Her hands were stuck in claw-like positions. She couldn't move them. She was sobbing.

My instinct was to comfort her. I was trying to be strong for her. My symptoms of shock were different than hers. I was still in disbelief.

*This can't be real. It's all just a bad dream, and I am going to wake up and it's going to all be fine.*

In my gut, I knew my daughter was dead but in my denial, I kept waiting for an EMT or paramedic to come over and tell us she was going to live.

I kept looking over at the huddle of medics and EMTs surrounding Rowyn, but I could no longer see her.

Cassie's hands trembled, covered in my daughter's blood. She rocked back and forth. I went to grab her hand, and she flinched back like she was afraid to touch me.

"Cassie, I don't blame you. This is not your fault. I love you," I said.

She was reluctant to believe me. She was waiting for me to blame her.

Wrapping my arms around her, we hugged for a long time in the grass, sobbing together and rocking back and forth.

Out of the corner of my eye, I saw someone running full speed toward us. I looked up and saw it was my cousin Robin. She was crying before she even reached us.

She wrapped her arms around me. "It's okay, it's okay. Who is it? Is it Rowyn?" she asked in a quivery voice.

I couldn't even speak through the lump in my throat, so I simply nodded.

We were all sobbing together by then. She was stroking my head, trying to comfort me, holding me like a baby on the ground.

"Where's Cody?" she finally asked, looking around the property that was filled with police and paramedics.

"I don't know, Robin." My voice shook around the words. "I think he's going to kill me. He hates me. . . and to be honest, I don't even care if he does."

As Cassie and I sat there together, still in our state of shock, a firefighter dressed in casual clothes walked over to us. He was a good family friend of my father-in-law, so knew our family fairly well.

I can't recall the exact words he used to tell us, but he was the one who told me my daughter was dead.

"Brynn, I'm so sorry to have tell you this, but she is no longer with us," he said with his head down.

To actually hear those words out loud was shocking.

"No, no, no. . . no, no." I was shaking my head, the devastation becoming clearer. "This *can't* be real! Is this real?"

In that moment, nothing at all mattered to me anymore.

I wanted to die.

I did not care about living any longer.

*What do I have to live for? My daughter is dead under my watch. This is all my fault. Everyone will hate me. My family and friends, how can anyone ever forgive me for letting this happen? Cody is going to shoot me, and that would be fine because I don't want to live any longer anyway. I just want to be with Rowyn.*

The firefighter reached for my hand and pulled me up to wrap his arms around me. "I am so, so sorry," he said.

In the arms of a firefighter who desperately tried to save my daughter, I cried, unable to process what just happened.

The police and detectives were taping off the scene. . . it looked just like a television show. Except this wasn't something I could just turn off; this was my front yard, reality's worst nightmare.

*This is not real. . . this cannot be really happening. . . my life is over. . . I want to die. . .*

As fast as I thought those words to myself, a strong female voice sternly said, "YOU are going to be okay! Everything is going to be just fine!"

I was baffled by where this inner voice came from. I stood there still in disbelief about everything that just happened, hearing a voice in my head. She sounded like an older woman watching over me. She was very convincing actually, because she did in fact give me some hope.

I was standing on my sidewalk sobbing only a few feet from Rowyn when I saw Cody's Aunt Cindy and cousin, Robin, coming toward me. They were both crying and embraced me.

I was weak in the knees and trembling. I felt like I was going to collapse at any moment.

Cindy pulled me close and held my face with both hands, just like I was her own child, "Now you listen to me, okay! This is NOT your fault. The last thing you need to do right now is blame yourself. Do you understand?"

Stuck in a trance of devastation, I just stared at her blankly. "It is my fault. I really think Cody is going to shoot me. . . and I don't even care."

I could see her trying to be strong and hold back the tears. She shook her head. "NO, listen to me. This is not your fault, okay? We will get through this as a family. Whatever you need, we are here, okay! We are not leaving you."

I was trying to process what she was saying. Everything seemed like it was in slow motion and confusing. Still filled with guilt and blame, I nodded to appease her.

Cody came blazing toward me. He looked weak, angry, and upset.

"Take off that bathrobe!" he snapped as he neared me. "You should look at yourself!"

I looked down at my chest soaked in blood. It looked so bad. *This is my daughter's blood.* I kept looking down in numbness.

I untied my robe and as I was slipping it off my shoulders, an officer standing nearby came over and grabbed it from me.

"I will discard of this for you," he said.

Revealing what I was wearing underneath, I felt completely exposed but I didn't care about anything at that point. I was wearing a thin T-shirt with no bra on and short, bedtime lounge shorts.

My husband glared at me with daggers in his eyes. I walked closer to him and reached my arms out to hold him.

His guard was up, but surprisingly, he let me. Wrapping my arms around him, I wanted his comfort. "I am so, so sorry, Cody. I can't believe this happened." I buried my head into his chest and sobbed.

His coldness turned into weakness as he put his arms around me and we cried together.

Our daughter, who we both cherished, laid on the ground deceased just a few feet from us. She had her favorite little blankie covering her up. It was teal mink fabric with little pink and coral birds on it.

Together, we walked over to her. Cody dropped to his knees on one side and I knelt down next to her on the other side. I grabbed her hand and held it, stroking her soft skin. Her hand was ghostly white but still slightly warm.

Cody rested his head on her chest. We were both crying, still in shock that any of this was real. It just couldn't be. Not us. Not my daughter

An EMT approached and informed us that we could spend some private time with our daughter in the ambulance if we wanted to. Of course we wanted to. I couldn't bear the thought of them taking her from me. I wanted to stay with her forever.

Cody scooped her delicate little body up.

"Don't look at her face!" I screamed through the sobbing as he lifted her up.

What I had seen earlier, I didn't want him to see. He had already seen it, too, but over the time that had passed, I saw her face was swelling and no longer looked like her beautiful self.

He carried her to the ambulance. I watched him walk with her slumped over his shoulder. It looked just like she was sleeping with her head rested on his shoulder. She was so tiny and precious.

I followed behind him with my head down, crying.

In the ambulance, Cody held her the whole time. I believe we spent many hours with her until they took her from us. I held her hands, stroking and kissing them. I stared at them, trying to take in the details of what they looked like because I knew I was never going to see them again. I loved her chubby little wrists with the rubber band rolls; her porcelain skin was so soft.

Cody and I would take turns rubbing her back as he held her still. Trying to comfort her like we normally would.

My father-in-law, Randy, and Cody's Uncle Rob joined us in the ambulance. They sat with us for a long time, just trying to keep their brave faces on for us.

Someone knocked on the ambulance door. Rob opened it and the detective requested to ask me some questions.

Cody was pissed. "Can you let us be with our daughter?"

I really didn't want to make anything harder than it already was, so I cooperated.

I stepped outside of the ambulance and shut the door.

I looked at my house, and strangers were just going in and out the front door. The door was wide open.

I looked back at the female detective as she was talking to me and really tried to concentrate on what she was saying. I was so confused.

I told her what had happened, for what seemed like the hundredth time.

She coldly kept asking about details of the morning.

*I know this is her job, but she's making me feel like a criminal. All I want is my daughter back.*

I complied the best I could until another officer came over. "I have already asked her everything. I can give you all the information," he said to her.

I was so relieved. He looked so familiar. . . I continued to look at him until I figured it out.

He was actually married to one of my friends from high school. They had two sons together, their youngest being around the same age as Rowyn.

I stepped over to him and hugged him. "Thank you," I said quietly.

I was so thankful to not have to repeat the whole story in detail again.

"You're welcome," he said, and I could see in his eyes that this was not easy for him, either.

I walked back into the ambulance and sat down next to Cody holding Rowyn. It didn't take long before another knock came to the door.

Randy opened it once again, and it was his friend. Randy nodded for him to come in and he stepped inside and took a seat. My mind was so disoriented and I was sure Cody's was, too.

He was talking to us, but I could not retain what he was saying. All I could compute out of it was that the coroner was there and we at some point would have to let her go.

I burst into tears again. "Where are they taking her? They can't take her away from me," I said through my chattering teeth. I was shaking and as hard as I tried to stop it, I couldn't. The trembling had taken over my body.

I didn't even like leaving her at daycare or her grandparents' for the day while I went to work, let alone the thought of some stranger driving off with her to the unknown.

This was every parent's worst nightmare.

I wanted to go with her.

*Is she going to be safe? Who is she going to be with? Are they going to put her little body in one of those coolers in the wall? I don't want her to be cold or scared.*

The thoughts overwhelmed me, and all I could do was sob. "NOOOO. . . no, no, no, no. . . I don't want her to go."

Uncle Rob, being a man of faith, asked if we would like a blessing over Rowyn's body.

We most definitely did. Cody laid Rowyn's delicate little body down onto the stretcher that was in the ambulance.

As he moved her, it was startling to see how her body reacted. . . not normal.

"Nooooooooo. . . oh, my God, don't look at her face, Cody!" I cried. "I don't want anyone to see her face."

Her face had become swollen and started to look bruised. It was horrible and beyond shocking to see.

I sobbed and shook so hard Randy put his hand on my shoulder to offer comfort. I could tell he didn't know what to do. I looked at him as my own father and I knew all he wanted was to be strong for us, but he was breaking down, too. We were all sobbing.

I knelt over and held Rowyn's hands. They were cold.

Cody covered her up with her favorite blankie. Rob stood and did his blessing over Rowyn's body as I continued to hold her hands. I was so disoriented that I really couldn't focus on what Rob was saying, but it did make me feel a little better. I knew my baby was in Heaven, but that didn't make it any easier to accept the fact that she was gone.

AFTER HOURS, WE KNEW it was time. They were going to take her away.

We stepped outside of the ambulance and our driveway was still lined with cars. It was like everybody was just waiting on us.

The female detective came back over to talk to me. "When you are ready, the coroner is going to take Rowyn's body," she said.

Nothing prepared me for that moment. Nothing at all. I was trembling even more than before, and I could not stop my teeth from chattering.

I hated what she'd just said to me. I was still trying to cooperate, but I really was not ready to let her go.

"Where are they taking her?" I asked.

In our conversation, another woman walked up. I didn't know who she was or who she worked for. She was much more comforting instead of the stiff detective.

The woman reassured me that they were going to take good care of Rowyn. She was going to be transported to Hawks Prairie, and that was where she would be until her funeral home was decided on.

I couldn't even respond; I just slowly nodded, still in disbelief.

As the team of medics took Rowyn's tiny little body from the ambulance, it seemed like another shockwave hit me.

I was weak in the knees and felt like I was going to collapse.

They loaded into the back of this big white truck. It had large doors that opened on the back like the ambulance did, with large storage compartments on the sides.

It disgusted me. It reminded me of a meat truck or something sick. It was just driving around with dead bodies in it.

I wanted to puke. Cody came over to me, crying, and I wrapped my arms around him.

I felt like he hated me, and I knew things would never be the same again.

He weakly put his arms around me as well, and we held each other as they put our baby in the back of this disgusting truck. It didn't seem to take that long before the truck was backing into our field to turn around.

I lost it. Cody and I sobbed together.

"Don't take her from me!" I was screaming. All I could manage after was repeatedly saying, "Nooooooooooooooo!"

I buried my face into Cody's chest as we both clung together, sobbing.

I wanted to fall on the ground and never get up.

Raising my head for a moment, I looked again at the white truck driving down our long gravel driveway. Anxiety overwhelmed me.

*I bet she is so scared. . . Is she cold? They better not put her in some little cooler in the wall. . .*

I was going to lose it at any moment. *They are going to have to put us into a looney bin. . . Who is going to take care of Wyatt for us?*

I looked around and saw my cousin, Courtney, crying and hugging her husband, Tray.

*Maybe they will take care of Wyatt for us.*

All these thoughts raced through my mind. I still wasn't sure if I was going to be arrested or not, or if I was going to the looney bin.

Either way, I didn't really care. I just wanted my baby back.

CASSIE

IS THIS A DREAM?

*"Even the smallest person can change the course of your future."*
*J.R.R. Tolkien*

I never thought I would ever be in this position, feeling this overwhelming sense of numbness to the point where I couldn't even draw in a breath, let alone speak clearly.

*This is a dream. It's not real,* I was thinking to myself as I dialed 911.

"Brynn, what's your address? Brynn, I need your address!" I shouted in pure panic.

I don't remember them saying, "911, what's your emergency?"

I don't remember explaining why we needed them.

I don't remember if I was speaking to a man or a woman.

All I knew was this could not be real. It just couldn't.

I couldn't be looking at my friend holding her daughter in her arms, who I ran over. *No, that couldn't be real.* It has to be a dream. It *is* a dream. "Is she breathing?" they asked me.

The thing was it *was* real. It was real to me, to Brynn, to Rowyn.

"Brynn, is she breathing?"

*Please, say yes. Let her be breathing!*

Brynn cradled Rowyn in her arms, standing on the front steps while shouting for Cody. "I don't know," she replied.

"Well, we have to find out," I said, my hands and body shaking.

Still on the phone, I scooped Rowyn out of Brynn's arms and immediately saw the red covering the front of Brynn's bright white robe.

Rowyn was bleeding. The gravity of the situation hit me like a punch to the heart. That was *her* blood on Brynn.

Carrying Rowyn to the grass, I laid her down carefully, all while holding the phone between my right shoulder and ear. Frantically, I felt for a pulse on her tiny pale neck, and I thought I had found a faint one.

"I don't know, maybe. I think so," I replied, merely inches from her face.

They instructed me how to begin CPR: tilt her head back, chest compressions and breaths.

I don't remember the instructions.

I remember counting out the compressions then giving her the breaths.

In the background, I could hear Cody running out of the house screaming, "Who the fuck is this? Brynn, who the fuck is this?"

"Cody, this is Rowyn!" I said in a panic. "I know you know how to give CPR to babies."

Cody jumped to action, and I continued to talk to the 911 operator.

"She's gone!" he said. "Her neck is already broken."

I kept doing the compressions and the breaths exactly as the operator said. I had no idea where Brynn was at that time or where Cody had went, but I couldn't stop. She wasn't gone to me; I had to save her. It just was not going to end that way.

"Someone should be there any second to take over," the operator said, and just as she said it, the first responder appeared.

He was a police officer. Kneeling beside me, he put some gloves on and took over.

In a daze, I put my hands behind my head and immediately thought of our two little boys still in the car.

Running over to them, I opened the door. "Are you boys okay?"

"Yah, what's happening?" they asked in scared little boy voices, and I noticed they were out of their car seats.

"Everything is going to be okay. Just stay in the car," I said.

Not knowing what else to do, I walked back to the grass toward Rowyn and called my husband.

He didn't answer.

I called again, and again there was no answer.

I tried the fourth time in a row, and finally got him on the line.

"Hello?" he answered.

"Aaron, come now!" My words rushed out in a breath, my hands barely able to hold the phone to my ear. "You gotta come now. I ran over Rowyn!"

I don't remember his response.

Brynn appeared. We couldn't even really look at one another.

"Cassie, this isn't happening. This is a dream," she said, her voice shaking around the words.

"I know, Brynn. This can't be happening. I can't even cry," I told her.

"Me, either. It's not real." she said.

Rowyn was behind us and somehow in that short time, many other first responders had arrived.

I don't remember how many ambulances, firetrucks and police cars were there, but there were a lot.

They were all working on her, desperately trying to save a life.

"What do we do?" I asked her, not knowing what else I could do. I'd just run over her daughter, a beautiful baby girl I adored. I was at a loss on how to fix this, because I had to, right? I could fix it, right?

The truth was I couldn't.

"Let's pray," she said. We were both already on our knees holding hands when she began with, "Heavenly Father, we need a miracle."

I don't remember the rest of the prayer.

What I do remember are the strangled words that constricted her throat and left in horrified shout. "Please, fix my baby!"

It was a prayer that went unanswered.

Within a few minutes, a female paramedic walked over to us and put her hands on our backs. "I'm so sorry. We have done everything we can do," she said softly, only to us.

That statement is forever engrained in my mind.

The tears that were not falling, the dream I felt like we were in, the foggy thoughts I had of spending the day at the hospital while she recovered, it all disappeared.

Rowyn was gone.

I don't remember how I transitioned from being on my knees next to Brynn to sitting cross-legged in the grass alone, but it happened.

I was alone. And that was exactly how I felt in those moments following the words, *"We have done everything we can do."*

I wanted to melt into the ground and disappear.

In that moment, my phone rang. It was still in the grass beside me since I had been speaking to the 911 operator. It was Aaron, so I answered and said, "She died, Aaron."

"No way," he replied, unable to believe the words.

"Yes, just hurry," I said, and we hung up.

Brynn and Cody's cousin, Robin, suddenly appeared at my side.

I don't remember what she said, or if I said anything to her, but I do remember her repeating to me, "It's not your fault. It's not your fault. It's not your fault."

But I couldn't believe her in those moments.

People started appearing, but nobody I knew, all police officers.

The scene played out before me like a horrible nightmare as I rocked forward and back. It was as if I was sitting in a fake rocking chair receiving comfort.

The scarf I was wearing that day, the one I didn't understand why I was wearing, was draped over my mouth soaked with tears, my sunglasses covering the downpour of emotion.

As people approached me, they all just put their hands on me—my back, my hand, my knee.

"What do I do?" I repeated probably a hundred times in those hours.

"You are smack dab in the middle of the worst day of your life, and there is nothing you can do," someone replied—who, I don't remember.

"Ma'am, is there anyone we can call for you?" they asked me, unknown faces wanting answers I couldn't give them.

"No," I replied.

Shamefully, I didn't want anyone to know. But I knew, eventually, they would. The whole world would know what I did.

It wasn't long before the questions started coming. Questions I never even thought someone would think to ask, let alone ask me.

They needed to know what had happened. I told them the story, and as I watched from a distance, my car was being surrounded with yellow tape. It was a crime scene. Had I committed a crime?

Photographs were being snapped of the scene when the questions came. "Cassie, I am sorry I have to ask you this, but

BRYNN JOHNSON | CASSIE MILLER

have you been drinking or using drugs this morning?" a police officer asked me.

"No," I replied, my stare fixated on the yellow tape.

"Was there anyone else in the car with you?"

"Our boys, and they are still in there," I said.

Immediately, the firefighters and police officers on the scene got the boys out of the car.

They kept them at a distance, trying to occupy them with the firetrucks.

"Ma'am, is there someone we can call to come and pick up your son for you?" someone asked.

"My nanny. She's home with my other son, but she's never driven my kids before." The irony of my statement made my tears fall harder.

I was concerned about her driving my boys, when I had just run over and killed my friend's baby.

With the numbness surrounding me, controlling my every motion of the day, I don't remember them making the call to Rachelle, our nanny, but it happened.

"I just feel like we need to call someone to come and be with you. Are you sure there is nobody we can call for you?" a first responder asked again, wanting to provide me with some sort of comfort.

"Just my work," I responded. "They need to know I won't be in today, and Little Seeds Preschool. . . the boys are supposed to be there."

Looking back, it is surprising this was even a concern of mine. It is certainly evidence of the shock I was in. The magnitude of the situation had only just begun to unveil itself.

The police officer took my phone and began dialing contacts I had told him about.

After a couple of tries to my boss and to Amy they couldn't get anyone to answer.

I told him to try Espen, another coworker. "Hi, Espen, this is Officer. . . " I don't remember his name, but he then went on to say, "We need to let you know that Cassie Miller will not be in to work today. She is currently detained."

*Detained? Me? I'm detained?*

I heard the word 'detained' and immediately wondered what he was thinking on the other end.

I realized then that I really could be going to jail.

It didn't matter to me if I did go to jail. I wanted to die right with Rowyn. I felt that I deserved to.

BEFORE TOO LONG, THERE was a chaplain beside me, as well as a detective. Prayers were being said and more questions on what had transpired were being asked.

A firefighter brought me wet wipes for my face and hands, as they still had some of Rowyn's blood on them.

"Ma'am, I know you are real shook up right now, but your son is really upset. He just wants to come over here to talk to you and see that you're all right."

"No," I said. No way could I have him over near me while I was in this condition.

By time, my hands no longer worked. They were in the shape of claws, and I couldn't move them. I was shaking as if it was below zero outside, and comforting my son was out of the question.

As hard of a thing as it was to say aloud, I just knew I couldn't be there for him in the middle of this. "My hands are stuck," I said.

"You are in a state of shock," someone replied.

Some family members of Brynn's appeared beside me, the chaplain still holding my hand and praying, and another detective arrived.

She wasn't as comforting, had more of a seriousness to her and went through a second round of questions.

I had no idea where Brynn and Cody were during that time, but in the distance I saw Cody's dad, his wife, and our boys walking around to the back of the house.

I was relieved; at least it was something to get Easton's mind off seeing me.

It sounds bad to say this now, but I had forgotten about my son after that point.

"What do we do?" I asked again to those around me.

No one had an answer for me, at least not one I remember hearing.

My husband arrived, finally.

We sat in the grass together with the chaplain and cried.

"I didn't mean to," I told Aaron, hoping he understood how truly sorry I was.

"I know," he said, gripping my hand.

The chaplain held both of our hands at the same time and continued to comfort us with prayer and warmth.

*What do we do?*

*What do I do?*

*What am I supposed to do?*
*What do I do?*

BRYNN

WHY ME GOD, WHY?

*I have made you and I will carry you. I will sustain you and I
will rescue you.*
Isaiah 46:4

"This can't be real! This feels like a nightmare, like it's not really happening," I said, a horrible dose of reality sinking in.

I watched the white oversized, unmarked county truck back into our field then turn around and head down my long, gravel drive with my daughter.

My legs were weak. I started screaming. I don't even think my words made any sense.

I was completely shutting down. I could barely stand as I embraced my husband and we sobbed together.

He held me up, but I felt as though we were both going to collapse any second. I was overcome with so many terrible emotions. Pain, guilt, worry, anxiety, fear.

*Nothing else matters. My daughter is dead, and nothing else matters to me.*

I wanted to die.

I lifted my head, which had been buried in Cody's chest. Everybody was watching us.

Our family was surrounding us and everybody was crying, waiting to see what we would do.

"Where is my mom?" I asked.

She was the only relative I had close by, the closest person to me, and she wasn't there.

Numerous people began speaking up and telling me they had been calling her and couldn't reach her.

I couldn't contain my tears. They just rolled down my face. "All I want is my mom," I cried.

I saw Aunt Cindy walk over to an officer still on scene. After she quietly talked to him, she came back over to Cody and me. "The officer is going to drive to your mom's house and pick her up."

*She must be sleeping.*

There was a huge lump in my throat and I could have honestly thrown up at any second, so I just nodded my understanding.

I didn't see Cassie or Aaron but from the last I saw of them, they seemed pretty unstable.

"Why don't you go take a shower and get cleaned up? When you're done, your mom should be here," Cindy suggested.

All I could manage to utter was, "Okay."

Staring at my reflection in my bathroom mirror was shocking. I looked like I had been in a horror movie. My hair

BRYNN JOHNSON | CASSIE MILLER

was soaked in my daughter's blood, now hours old so it had formed little dreadlocks.

My face was beet red and blotchy from crying, and I looked like I had stepped right out of Hell.

I stripped my clothes off and heard a light knock at the door.

"Brynn, it's Sheri. Can I come in?" I really just wanted to be alone and collapse to the shower floor and sob, but I responded yes for her to come in.

She slid the bathroom door open, and her expression seemed a little shocked to my fully exposed body. I just didn't care. I normally would not be comfortable standing buck naked in front of anyone, but I really could not care about anything at all.

*Who cares about being naked when I just witnessed my daughter's death?*

I turned on the shower and Sherie sat on the edge of the jet tub.

I knew why she was there; she didn't trust me to be by myself. "I'm okay, you don't have to be in here."

*She must think I'm going to try to kill myself or something.*

"I just want to make sure you're okay. . . I don't want you to be alone up here in case you need anything," she said.

"Okay. I swear, I will be fine, but okay."

Would I, though? I felt so weak.

My hand was shaking as I opened the shower door and slid in. I stuck my face in the hot water. I wanted to just fall down to the ground.

*I hate my life now! What the hell just happened, God?! This is not real, is it?*

"I really don't know what's real right now. Is this really happening, Sheri?" I asked.

"I know. It doesn't seem like it's real. . . I'm so sorry," she said.

I reached my hands back to wash my hair, and all I could feel were clumps of hair stuck together from blood.

I looked down and red was rolling down my chest into the drain.

"I could puke." I felt so dirty and disgusting. Like a horrible human being.

*I just can't believe this is really happening to me. My baby is gone!!*

"Let me help you." Sheri opened the shower door and started separating my hair.

I was so weak I could barely lift my arms to wash my hair myself. She lathered up some shampoo and started doing it for me.

I stayed in the shower for a long time, until the water was getting cold.

Sheri stayed with me the whole time.

As I got out of the shower, she wrapped me in a towel like I was her toddler. I scuffed over to my closet, fell to the floor and cried.

I was living my worst nightmare, and I hated my life.

SITTING WITH MY KNEES pulled to my chest, I was rocking back and in forth. The tears just would not stop coming.

I had been in my closet for hours. It was where I felt the safest. My place in the house. Rowyn played in my closet every morning while I was getting ready.

Just the day before, I was frustrated with her because she was running through my closet, pulling down anything she could reach while laughing.

I would never hear her laughter again or be able to get ready with her in the mornings.

*Why, Lord? Why me? I don't understand! I try so hard to be a good person and I'm a believer, and this is what my destiny is! You take my daughter?!*

I was heartbroken and pissed at the same time. I was so confused I couldn't focus on all the emotions I was feeling.

"Brynn?" I heard Cindy quietly call my name.

"Yes, you can come in." Cindy and my cousins Robin and Niki came in.

Cindy had made me a plate of food. "Here, you really need to eat something. I just made a few things for you." She held the plate in front of me as if trying to entice me to either eat or come out of the closet.

"I can't eat. . . I feel so sick, I could throw up." My nausea hadn't gone away. I was shaky and felt queasy.

Before I knew it, more girls were crowded into my bathroom, just staring down at me as I still sat in my safest place, the closet.

It was mostly family and a few of my closest friends. Everyone was staring at me.

*I don't even know how to function right now.* I just continued to rock back and forth like a crazy person.

*I probably will have to go to a crazy-person hospital or something. Don't really care, though. I'm sure I belong there.*

Over what seemed like a long time, and after repeatedly reassuring the girls that I would be fine by myself, everyone finally went back downstairs.

I grabbed whatever was on top of the comfy pile and finally dressed myself. Stepping out of my closet into the bathroom, I stared at my hideous reflection in the mirror. I was almost unrecognizable to myself. I didn't know the weak, ghostly pale, hideous person in the mirror.

*Who have I become, and who am I going to be now?*

Again, I felt the emotions taking over me. I started hysterically crying, shuffling to the closet before I fell to the floor again. I started praying for a long time. I spoke out loud. I was trying not to be angry with God, but how could I not?

I was open, raw and honest with him. "How could you let this happen to my baby, God? I don't understand. I try so hard to be the best mother I can be, the best person I know how to be! I adore my children! And mine is killed in my driveway!"

Rage was rearing its ugly head.

I sobbed and just wanted to punch something. I was so angry I wanted to completely destroy anything in my path. But I was honestly too weak to get off the floor.

My rage quickly turned back into the brokenness. "Why, why, why, Lord? I don't understand. Please, comfort me, Lord, and wrap your loving arms around me. I don't know how my family and I will ever overcome this, but please give us some comfort." I prayed by myself and continued to sob for a long time until I had this urge to go downstairs.

I had no idea what time it was, nor did I care, but something was comforting me in that moment. It took all of my energy to pick myself up and wipe my face from all the tears. I somewhat composed myself and decided it was time to go downstairs. I had been hiding a long time, but I missed Cody and wondered how he was. Something was almost encouraging me to go downstairs.

SLOWLY, I MADE MY way, feeling as though my legs were going to give out at any moment, so I held the banister as I went. I could see through the large window facing out toward the driveway that a ton of cars were still there.

There was a man I had never seen before approaching the house. I paused my steps as I watched him coming toward my home. He looked nervous but filled with strength at the same time.

That urging feeling came upon me again, and something was telling me to go outside and meet this strange man. I continued to make my way down the stairs and went straight out the front door. I stared at him and was filled with a little bit of peace and comfort.

I didn't know what was pushing me forward, but I continued walking toward him. I met him on the sidewalk that led to my home, only a few feet away from where my daughter just was.

He started to introduce himself. "You don't know me, but a friend of mine had asked me to come here. My name's

Jim Ford, and I am the pastor at the New Day Christian Center right down the road from here."

As he was talking to me, I was putting the pieces together on who he was and where the connection was coming from. I recognized his name as soon as he said it.

I remembered hearing the story of his daughter passing a few years back. It was also a tragic accident. The story always stuck with me, and I often had thought of their family over the years. I gave him the biggest hug and didn't want to let go.

"I know who you are," I said.

He hugged me back, like the way a dad would comfort his own daughter.

For some reason, just having that connection with him seemed to help comfort me a little bit. I felt like I could completely trust him.

After all, he was a parent who knew what I was feeling right then. I knew God had sent him to me. He was an answer to my prayer from just minutes before.

Any bit of comfort and hope I could receive. . . and it arrived on my doorstep.

PASTOR JIM STAYED QUITE a while. I saw him and Papa Randy out in the driveway talking. I knew he needed comfort just as much as I did. His grandbaby just died. She was his only girl in the family and his everything. I felt so bad. I have never seen him cry, and now all I could see was him from behind, sitting on a tailgate of someone's truck with his head down in his hands.

I love him as my own father, and he has always been my rock through anything and everything. Papas were supposed to be strong, but who could be strong in this situation?

I was roaming aimlessly around, looking for Cody. I finally found him wandering around outside. It felt like a whole day since I had seen him. He also looked like hell, distraught, confused, beaten down and angry.

When he saw me, he still had this bit of fire in his eyes, like he hated me for what had happened. I didn't blame him one bit. I wasn't sure that, if the roles had been reversed in our situation, I could forgive him for letting anything happen to our baby girl.

Without saying a word, he reached out his arm and motioned for me to come in for a hug.

The fire faded and we hugged. As soon as he wrapped his arms around me, we both started crying again. It was like we took on each other's pain as we held one another. I could only imagine how he must have been feeling right then. We were sobbing so hard that we were shaking. I just buried my head in his chest and wanted the nightmare to be over.

"Hey, kids, I really think you should go have a private talk with the pastor," Randy said as he walked toward us. "He really made me feel better, and I think it would be beneficial for both of you to talk to him."

I had so many questions and thoughts racing through my mind. I wanted nothing more than to talk to him.

I was desperate for any sense of comfort I could get.

I looked up at Cody as if waiting for him to make the decision for both of us. "Yeah, I'll talk to him," he said.

We walked over to the tailgate where Randy had previously been. An odd place to receive a counseling session, but with all the people around it seemed like the only place for us to have some privacy.

Jim's appearance wasn't what you typically picture a pastor looking like. He was dressed very casually, wearing jeans and Converse sneakers. He even had his ear pierced.

He was very laid-back and approachable, but his passion for Christ definitely shone brightly.

He answered all of our questions. Some I was sure were not easy for him at all, but he was the rock we needed at the time.

He prayed over us. I could feel the peace and strength radiating off him as he put his hands over me in prayer.

*Wow! I have never felt God's presence like that before.*

His words offered both Cody and I comfort, as well as hope and faith that we knew where Rowyn was. She was safe in the arms of God in Heaven.

I could tell by Cody's reaction to Jim's words that he was also feeling a small bit of relief. I believed everything he said, and I clung to it. He reassured us that he would always be there for us no matter what or when. . . and I knew he would be.

## CASSIE

### MAKE IT STOP

*The struggle you're in today is developing the strength you need for tomorrow. – Author Unknown*

Sitting tearful and numb, amongst all of the uniforms and nameless faces, an officer approached us in the grass and said, "You guys are free to go when you are ready, but we need to keep your car here a little longer for the investigation."

"Okay," Aaron said.

Just then, I saw Cody, without a shirt, and he walked over to me in the grass.

Leaning down, he hugged me as I sat on the grass. It only made me cry harder. "I am so, so sorry."

"I know," he calmly whispered, and then walked off toward the back of his house.

*I can't be here any longer.*

"I wanna go home." I said, looking at Aaron.

We stood up together, and holding my hand we began to walk across the lawn. Just feet away from where Rowyn once laid in the gravel on the right, and where I was doing CPR on her to the left.

I didn't even notice it at the time, but I was dragging my purse on the ground. I apparently had no energy to carry it. The officers had brought it to me to get my driver's license for the investigation.

Seeing what I was doing, my husband picked it up off the ground and carried it for me.

We walked past the ambulance that I later learned Rowyn had spent the last three hours being held by her parents in.

Just past it, I saw our friends Courtney and Tracy— relatives of Brynn and Cody—had arrived on the scene.

Immediately, I latched onto both of them and cried. There were no words to say that would change any of this. "I'm so sorry."

To me, it felt very quiet and very different from the chaos I felt just moments before. Courtney and I hugged the longest, but I do not recall the words we exchanged.

We finally walked over to Aaron's little white commuter Toyota, and I climbed in the passenger seat.

Glancing to the left, I saw the first responders' vehicles one last time, but some had already left the scene unnoticed. One vehicle in particular stood out to me.

It was a small version of the newer-looking Fed Ex trucks. It was tiny, white and unmarked. It was the coroner.

I don't remember how or why I knew it was the coroner; possibly I saw her being moved into it, but I honestly have no recollection of it.

That vehicle, to this day, is a horrific flashback that I have.

I never did see Brynn again, and I still don't know where she was when I left her house that day.

As my husband reversed and we started to pull off down their long driveway, I glanced out the window. On the right, in the tall brush, I saw Cody.

He was alone, looking up toward the sky, before he fell to his knees.

I will never forget seeing that.

It was heartbreaking and unbearable. Seeing anyone standing there in that situation just hours after losing their baby girl, but then to be the person driving the car that took her life? It broke me, and I continued to cry and bury my face in my scarf.

As we approached the end of their driveway, the phone rang and Aaron answered it. "Okay, we'll wait for you to leave before we go home."

It was his parents; they were at our house packing up clothes for our kids to take them back to their house. Aaron must have spoken to them before he got to the scene. Then my mom called his phone.

"Yeah," he answered. "We're headed back to the house now. Are you guys headed over? Okay, we'll see you about 3:30 then."

"Is that my mom?" I asked.

"Yeah," he said.

"Let me talk to her," I responded.

My mom sounded shook up when she said, "Hi, baby."

My parents at that time had been living at my grandma's, taking care of her at night because she was beginning her rapid decline from pancreatic cancer.

"Mom, don't come," I said. "Grandma needs you more. I'll be okay."

She wasn't having that. "Cassie, we are coming and we will see you soon," she said in a stern, worried tone. As I hung up, Aaron had turned down some road I had never been on before. I looked up to him, and without even asking why he explained we were killing time so the kids would not be there when we got back. I was barely able to look out the window; my face just felt more comforted buried in the scarf. "I didn't mean to," I said to him.

"I know, it was just a tragic accident," he responded.

Even still, I was rocking back and forth crying. You really do not know where all of the tears could possibly come from, but they never dried up.

We got back on the main road of 183$^{rd}$ and passed his parents driving off with our kids.

I couldn't even look up to wave at their Jeep.

We pulled up to the house, but I have no recollection of the short walk from the car inside. I just remember the house was as empty and quiet as I felt on the inside. Walking straight to my bedroom, I got completely undressed and sat down in the shower with the hot, steamy water pouring over my head.

I was numb.

Washing off every last bit of the scene from my face and hands, it still didn't feel real.

Aaron came in and asked, "Do you need anything?"

"Call Jen," I said. "Tell her what has happened."

I knew the word would start to spread through the town quickly, but I wanted her to hear it from us. She was Rowyn's babysitter, and I knew she would be heartbroken, as well. I also knew she would notify my other friends.

As Aaron made the call, I climbed out of the shower and put on sweatpants and a blue hoodie. Wet hair, shivering, and straight-faced, I climbed into my bed and lay there alone.

It wasn't long before I received a text from my friend Becka. It wasn't anything about the accident, just a normal message. I simply responded that something very bad had happened and I had run over my friend's baby and she died. I asked that she please tell my other friends. I couldn't even type that message without breaking down again. It was like facing the reality of the situation when I typed it.

Before long, Courtney and Jennifer Johnson—both relatives of Brynn and Cody—arrived at my bedside. They had returned my car from the scene.

We hugged, we cried, and in my messy dark bedroom, they comforted me.

"I'm not worried about Rowyn," Courtney said to me. "I know she is good to go, but I am worried about you."

It was probably the first time I had heard her share anything, in the seven years I had known her, that let me know she was strong in her faith.

At that point, I was clueless of what this could possibly mean because I was not strong in my faith that day.

Honestly, picturing Rowyn as 'good to go' after I had tried desperately to save her seemed incredibly generous to say.

Not long into this visit, the revolving door began. All of my other friends started piling in.

We cried, and together I told them what had happened. They got me outside on the patio at the table, and I felt like I spent several days there.

Around 3:30, my parents arrived, and I walked to the door and grabbed onto my dad. I wept harder than I had since I'd been home. I told him what had happened, just kept saying, "I didn't mean to do it."

"I know," he said, crying along with me.

My mom appeared in the corner of my eye and we couldn't even speak to one another, just held onto each other and wept.

Floral arrangements, food platters, gifts, and people began to fill my empty home that afternoon. It was a day of grieving for many, but for me it was still very unbelievable. It was still a day of shock.

Friends brought me some of my favorite things, corndogs and Red Vines licorice. People prepared dinners for us for a couple of weeks. All around me, everywhere I looked, people were just there, doing things without being asked to.

I may have felt empty as all hell on the inside, but I had love and support like no other on the outside. I walked out toward the chicken coop with my dad that evening, and I couldn't stop shivering. I didn't understand it because it wasn't cold. He told me it was shock.

I remember one thing that he told me specifically that day that I think about quite often. "You hold your head up high," he said, "and do not worry about what anybody says."

It sounded impossible. I already had fears of what would be said, and holding my head up after that was not going to be easy.

# Chapter Thirteen

## CASSIE

### I'M ALIVE BUT IT DOESN'T FEEL LIKE IT

*"Grief is like the ocean: It's deep, dark and bigger than all of us. And pain is like a thief in the night. Quiet. Persistent. Unfair. Diminished by time and faith and love." -Unknown*

When I came out of my bedroom the day after the accident, I couldn't tell if I had slept or not.

My parents and Aaron were in the kitchen, and my mom was making breakfast.

"Morning," they said, both gauging my reactions.

"Morning," I replied, blank-faced and numb.

*What am I supposed to do? Today, tomorrow, the next day? What is my life like now?*

Facing reality seemed like something I wasn't ready to do. I went back into my bedroom and climbed in my bed. I wasn't sure what to do, what to think about, and I had no idea how I was going to live. Wondering how I made it through the day before, I replayed images in my head.

Just then, I remembered I had a text from my boss. She had texted me that morning telling me she had sent me an email. She had given me the phone number for the Employee Assistance Program (EAP), and encouraged me to call them. She said she would get some forms to me to complete with a doctor to get some shared leave started. I barely had any leave at all because I had come off maternity leave in February, and I was saving what I could between sick kids and doctor appointments for time with my grandma, who was gravely ill with pancreatic cancer.

The first place I called was the Tumwater Family Practice, where I explained my situation for needing an appointment as soon as possible. They were incredibly sweet on the phone and got me in that morning. I knew that I was going to need some medication to make it through the upcoming months, and that taking my friend's Xanax the night before was not going to be in my best interest. I needed my own medication and my own evaluation.

I called the EAP next, and they got my husband and me in on that Thursday.

Here I was sitting on my bed—Wednesday morning after the accident—and if it wasn't for the Tumwater Family Practice clinic, I would have absolutely no idea what I was supposed to do.

But I knew I had to be at that doctor's office, so I had to get dressed. I took a shower and sat down again, unknowing how I was supposed to feel. I was incredibly sad, but by that time there were not tears. My face was extremely sore from all the muscles tightening as I cried. I climbed off the bed to see

I'd received a text message from one of my very best friend's mom, Wanda. She texted me to wear blue.

I was so glad to have gotten that little message from her, because standing before a closet full of clothes was enough to make me melt into the ground sobbing. I couldn't make a decision if my life depended on it, and I did not care about something as silly as clothes at that point. The thought kept crossing my mind, *How can I worry about what to wear today when I killed someone yesterday?*

I climbed into my mom's car in the passenger seat. It was the first time I had been in a car since the drive home the day before. I was anxious, and I felt like the smallest person in the world sitting in that seat. Almost like a little child.

It didn't take long before I experienced my first trigger.

My mom, driving cautiously, hit the slow-down rivets in the road and it threw me over the edge. I couldn't stop crying and rocking back and forth. My mom kept asking compassionately, "What is wrong?"

"The bumps," I muttered between sobs. "Rowyn was a bump."

When we arrived at the doctor appointment, I sat in the waiting room for just a minute before they called me back. Once in the room, I bawled in the chair hysterically, receiving hugs and words of faith from the nurse, doctor, and the appointment clerk.

She even brought me an envelope with the story of Christian musician Steven Curtis Chapman, who had been through a similar accident to us.

By the time I left, I had a very high dose of antidepressants and a Xanax prescription to help manage my mind.

I was a bit nervous about leaving because I knew Aaron and my dad would be home with my kids. It was a really tough thing to feel because I desperately wanted to hold my babies considering, but I was extremely afraid because I was so unstable.

When I walked into the house, I was greeted by my four-year-old son hugging me so hard.

"Mom, why were you crying? I missed you so much," he said.

It was heartbreaking.

Easton has always been so protective of me and intuitive to my feelings. I just told him I was sad, but that everything was going to be okay. My youngest, just nine months old, of course showed excitement to see me. However, I could not have imagined caring for him by myself during this time.

That afternoon, my house continued to be a revolving door. I think everyone wanted to do something, but nobody knew what.

People would say to me, "Is there anything I can do for you?"

My response was always the same: "I wish there was, but no."

I knew I was on a journey through no-man's land. I knew it had probably happened before to a couple of unfortunate loving mothers somewhere, but I did not know anyone personally who could help me through what I was facing.

Among the friends and family on the back patio, I sat listening to all of the conversations taking place, chiming in at times when I would forget for one split second what was going on.

I would immediately feel guilty that I forgot in that split second. I felt guilty when even for a moment I didn't feel the suffering. I didn't want to smile, although it was the most natural thing I ever did. It was hard to want to feel pain, but it was hard to also hold a conversation that wasn't related to Rowyn passing. Carrying a normal everyday conversation in light of the circumstances felt wrong.

That evening, I was putting pajamas on Easton, and he asked, "Mommy, are you going to die?"

"No, honey. Mommy isn't going anywhere, but how come you asked me that?" All I could wonder was what he had seen. All I could feel was incredible guilt for putting him in that situation. I was supposed to protect him for everything, and now he feared me dying.

"Did Rowyn die?"

"Yes, baby, she did. Mommy is going to buy a book that we can read together to explain some of this to you, but Rowyn is in Heaven now. She is an angel." I kept it together as I said it, but it was very hard. My little boy didn't know anything about Heaven or angels. As I said before, we were not Bible readers or church-goers.

He looked at me with confused eyes. "I really missed you, Mom."

"I know," I whispered. Then I brought him in my room and we snuggled in my bed to sleep together.

Again, I am unsure if sleep really took place that night either, but it was nice to have the comfort of my son with me. I knew that much.

The next day, I woke up knowing I had one plan for the day, and that was the EAP appointment. I received the text from Wanda again, telling me to wear pink.

We were to be meeting with a counselor there to help us somehow, but I really didn't know how. I would have accepted help from anyone who gave me hope at that point.

Aaron and I left early in my mom's car with the intention of going to the nursery down the road from our house. It was my mom's idea to buy a tree for Brynn and Cody to plant in honor of Rowyn.

We arrived at the nursery, though no one was there to assist us. I wandered around looking at everything they had, but it just wasn't right.

Unable to find what I was looking for, we decided to go to The Barn, a nursery in Tenino.

Immediately, we were greeted by a woman willing to help us find a tree.

We looked at several different ones, and there were a couple we were trying to decide between. I loved the weeping cherry tree, but I hated the name. It made me cry to even say the word 'weep'.

Eventually, I just burst into tears. I told the lady who I was. "I am the woman who ran over the baby on Tuesday, and I need to buy a tree for her parents, if you could please help us decide," I said, hoping she made sense of my words.

Making any sort of decision, large or small, was entirely too hard.

With her empathy and guidance, we went with the weeping cherry tree, as it would blossom each year close to Rowyn's birthday, and it would stay small like her.

My husband handed me a card to write in, and all I can remember it saying was, "I'm so so so so so so so so so sorry."

What do you say to the people whose daughter you ran over and killed? Words didn't seem like they would ever do justice. Words still don't seem like enough, but it was because they weren't. There would never be anything that was enough.

I cried so hard during this whole experience as it was incredibly painful, but the people at The Barn offered to deliver the tree for us for free, which was so generous.

We left there and spent the next two and a half hours with a counselor. We cried, I told the story, and described how I felt about myself. We also discussed the accident Aaron had witnessed just a month prior at his job-site. How some of the feelings he had endured could help him understand some of what I was feeling.

When we left there, she was going to be in touch with a therapist who would contact me to set up an appointment. I had no idea that the lady who would be contacting me would turn out to be someone who, in many ways, helped save my life.

At that point, I still had nothing to grab onto. I had called out to God and asked for his help, fell to my knees and begged Jesus Christ to come into my heart, but I still felt I had nothing. It was difficult because I knew I needed something, knew I needed the strength to come from somewhere, but I had no idea what it would look like when it came. I didn't even understand what I was asking for.

THE NEXT DAY WAS Friday, the third day since the accident. I got the text from Wanda, telling me to wear another color. My good friend Elder had arranged with us the night before to take the car away. She left hers with us in case we needed it, and she brought some printouts of new ones for me to look at.

As anyone could imagine, I could barely ride in a car at that point, so looking for a new one was not something I wanted to do at all. But I had no choice, because I had to get the other one off my property. I could not stomach to look at it.

I picked one off the sheet, and away she went to make a deal. She brought back the paperwork and I signed where she told me to. The car would be ready for us later the following week.

It didn't matter, since I couldn't drive anyway, but talk about a good friend. Nobody enjoyed wheeling and dealing with a car dealership, yet she spent a lot of her own time handling this for us so we didn't have to.

I had exchanged some texts daily back and forth with Brynn since Tuesday, mostly just us checking on one another.

Our husbands, Aaron and Cody, were also exchanging text messages. We were all four stuck in a fog, just going through the motions. They had said they wanted to come over, that they had left the house for the first time and were out making Rowyn's funeral arrangements.

We were nervous. Of course, we were grateful they didn't hate me, but we were nervous to see them.

They came in the house, giving us hugs and asked if we could talk with them in a separate room.

Brynn, Cody and I went into Easton's bedroom for some privacy. As we sat on his bed, I remember Brynn saying, "I can't explain it and I don't understand it myself, Cassie, but I love you more now than I did before. If it wasn't you and it was anybody else, I would have gotten my gun and killed them. I am glad it was you, because I know how much you loved my daughter." Their composure and compassion toward me was unbelievable, and the fact they chose not to blame but offer forgiveness showed exactly what kind of people that they are. Aaron and I have had that conversation numerous times. They are genuinely whole-heartedly good people.

Here they had been making the arrangements all day for their daughter, and then they were at my house telling me they loved me more. They didn't stay long, just enough to connect with us and then they left.

Brynn told us the burial would be on Monday and she really hoped I could come, but understood if I couldn't. Following that would be her celebration of life at the Jensen's Barn. I knew I had already been through the absolute worst day of my entire life on Tuesday.

But I realized I would be going through the second worst day of my entire life on the upcoming Monday.

That whole season, my husband and I had been coaching our son's U6 soccer team. It was our first experiences as coaches, and our first game was that night.

I couldn't go. I knew I could *not* go.

My family tried to encourage me to go, but I just could not face the Tenino public yet. I stayed behind at home while everyone went to the game. It was the first time I was alone, and it was really hard.

That evening, my best girlfriends from growing up had gathered from all over the state and came over. I can't even tell you how many people or who was at the house these last several nights, but we had a lot.

Friends would take on meal duties, snacks were constantly around, and my mom was caring for my children and my house.

Everyone stuck very close to us as we endured what I consider the worst pain possible.

# Chapter Fourteen

**BRYNN**

## WHAT THE HELL IS HAPPENING?

*"When you go through deep waters. I will be with you."*
*Isaiah 43:2*

I was pacing around in the yard looking for him when he came barreling through the crowd like a man on a mission. His eyes were glazed over and he was storming toward me like a lunatic.

I was scared.

*This is it. He's going to shoot me here in front of everyone.*

I started walking toward him, crying. All I wanted to do was hold my husband and cry.

I wanted to comfort him, and I *needed* him to comfort me.

"Get away from me," the lowness in his voice sent a chill through me.

"Cody, what are you doing?" I cried.

He stomped up the front porch stairs. "I'm getting my gun!" he yelled as he went in the house.

I looked around and all eyes were on me. I told the EMTs and police that were standing nearby that I thought my husband was either going to shoot me or himself.

Honestly, at that point, I didn't care one bit if he shot me.

I heard the sound of helicopters flying above the house.

Cody came storming out with a shotgun in his hands and pointed it up at the sky. He cocked the gun and started firing rounds into the air.

"NOOOOO!" I started screaming. "What are you doing? You're going to go to jail! I *need* you, please don't do that!"

He didn't give a shit what I was saying, nor do I think he heard me.

He was raging, screaming, pissed. He'd just lost his baby girl.

He kept firing rounds into the air, yelling like a mad man.

I put my head down and walked into the house. I couldn't control him, and I didn't blame him for being furious.

How dare they come hovering over our home, taking pictures and recording our daughter's death?

What an invasion of our privacy. We didn't get a call to ask permission.

My whole family was grieving after this tragedy and helicopters were flying over filming it.

I was honestly too exhausted and heartbroken to stir up a fit myself. I just didn't want him to shoot down a chopper and go to jail.

I stood in the kitchen in a daze. Cody's cousin, Erin, and Aunt Cindy cleaned the house in a whirlwind all around me. I think it was a comfort for them, as well.

"Brynn, I can call and make the news crews go away. Do you want me to do that?" Erin asked.

I was too exhausted to even give her an answer, so I just nodded.

That quick, she was on her cell phone talking to someone, and she sounded stern and walked out the front door. *This chick knows how to get things done.*

Within minutes, the choppers were out of there.

She came back in the house with a smile on her face. "All taken care of!" she said.

I have no idea who she called or what she said, but they were gone and I was relieved I wasn't going to hear gunshots and choppers outside anymore.

MY SENSE OF TIME seemed to blur. I had no idea what day it was, or even the month for that matter. I would ask about both multiple times a day.

Our family didn't leave our side. We had an inflatable mattresses throughout the house, and we also had relatives sleeping on couches. I hid in my closet and just cried. I couldn't possibly take care of Wyatt, let alone myself.

I couldn't eat, didn't want to live. I had no touch of reality anymore.

That night was treacherous. I was so afraid. I felt as though the Devil had just invaded my home and all my loved ones lives and would strike again at any moment. I lay in bed with my eyes wide open, just staring into the darkness.

I was waiting for the Devil to walk down the hallway.

He was winning.

He had taken my whole world in a matter of seconds and turned it upside-down.

I was terrified, and that was what the Devil wanted. He sought to destroy, kill, and ruin everything in his path.

My family was in his path, and I was terrified he would strike again.

Reaching over, I turned on the bedside light and scanned the room.

I jumped out of bed and rushed down the hallway to check on Wyatt. He was sleeping safe and sound with his auntie.

I left the hallway light on and peeked into Rowyn's room.

When I flipped on the light, I expected to see her standing in her crib, smiling at me. Of course, she wasn't there, but it still didn't feel real. She couldn't really be gone, could she? Wasn't this all just some sick nightmare?

I was afraid to tell Cody my thoughts. I knew I was losing it; I would have horrible visions as soon as I would close my eyes.

I was truly scared to go to sleep. As soon as I would doze off from exhaustion, I would have the worst nightmares or flashbacks of the accident.

I went back to my bed and decided to leave the lamp on for the night. I started to pray aloud. I just wanted these images to be gone from my mind.

"Lord, please keep my family safe, and please protect my little boy. I cannot handle anything else at this point. Lord, keep the Devil out of my home." I begged in my prayer for protection.

I needed all the help I could get. I was on the verge of a mental breakdown, and I knew it.

MY FIRST OUTING WAS a few days following the accident. Sheri had arranged a meeting at the funeral home.

Preparing to leave the house seemed like it took me hours. I couldn't keep focused long enough to even pick out something to wear.

I still could puke at any minute, and my anxiety was terrible. I felt reckless, like leaving the house I was a hazard to other people. I had no control over my emotions or my actions. I honestly could've snapped at any moment.

Sheri helped me get ready. All I wanted to wear was comfy clothes; I didn't care what I looked like. I heavily medicated myself with Xanax to try to calm my nerves. I was a wreck.

*I am going to a funeral home to start planning my daughter's funeral.*

Given my mental state, I couldn't comprehend what was happening. I was just going through the motions that people were telling me to.

Within about fifteen minutes, I started feeling fuzzy and calm from the pills. Still full of anxiety, but it did take the edge off.

Cody and I loaded into the car with Sheri, Randy, and my mom and headed to the dreaded funeral home.

As we pulled in, I checked out the nicely manicured grounds and the building. It was immaculately clean and pretty.

*Sad that's how these people make a good living. . . catering to dead people.*

I felt weak still, and I didn't want to get out of the car. Everybody unloaded and I was hesitating leaving the vehicle.

*I really don't want to do this.*

Cody helped me out of the car and we slowly walked together toward the funeral home entrance. As we headed inside, the woman at the front desk greeted us and said she would let Trent know we had arrived.

"Please, follow me," the receptionist said and started walking us down the hallway to a private room.

The room had a large conference-style table in it. There was a large television screen mounted on the wall, as well as shelving with displays of anything and everything you could purchase to represent your deceased loved one.

The place was very neat and tidy, but I was disgusted by being there. I wondered if my daughter's body was there somewhere.

*Is there like an oversized cooler somewhere, preserving bodies before their funerals? I wonder if they have a garage where they park the hearse.*

My mind raced with thoughts as Trent entered the room.

He introduced himself and shook all of our hands. He was very professional. He had dark hair, wasn't very old, maybe in his mid-30's, and he was wearing slacks and a button-up shirt.

He seemed very timid at first.

*This must not be a very easy job.*

I couldn't imagine having to talk to people about planning funerals or worse, embalming bodies.

As he explained the whole process of what we needed to do step by step, I started to zone out. I could not focus on what he was saying. All I managed to do was nod and try to pretend as though I knew what was going on.

He slid a large three-ring binder across the table to Cody and me. It was already opened to the infant casket page. I just stared at it.

*I have to pick one of these out? They are so ugly.*

There was only a limited selection of three caskets to choose from, and they all disgusted me.

Cody was silent also as we stared at the page. I knew he was thinking the same thing as me.

"Do you have any others we could look at?" I asked.

"No, unfortunately, this is all we have that comes in the size you need," Trent said.

"Hmmm, okay." I continued to stare at the page with the hideous casket options for my baby.

I wanted an extravagant turquoise one with a big bow on it or something over-the-top Rowyn. She was way too special to have an ordinary white or black casket.

It just didn't seem like that was good enough for her.

We decided to think about it for a while before making any decisions. When he started discussing cost, I couldn't even comprehend what he was talking about. I didn't want to think about it anymore, nor could I handle confining the tears much longer.

I wanted to get out of there. I have no idea how long we were there, but I was ready to leave.

Sheri left the room with Trent for a while. I was so thankful someone else was handling all the questions and decisions right then.

I was officially shut down and couldn't focus if I tried.

A<small>FTER LEAVING THE FUNERAL</small> home, Cody and I really wanted to see Cassie and Aaron. The only communication we had with them since the accident was through text message. I had already told Cassie that I didn't blame her, but she didn't believe me. I knew they weren't doing well, either.

I needed to tell Cassie again that I didn't blame her. I knew she was suffering. She was waiting for me at any moment to tell her I hated her and blame her for everything. I didn't. The Devil was attacking her home, too.

I didn't want her to go off the deep end. She was a mother and a wife, too.

Sheri drove us there and my anxiety was through the roof, so I took another Xanax to calm my nerves.

We pulled up to her home and there were lots of cars parked in her driveway.

I wasn't sure my legs would support me, and I felt so weak. I was afraid to see people. I didn't know who was inside.

We walked in and it was very quiet and solemn. Cassie and Aaron's parents were there and gave us a warm welcome.

Aaron's mom gave me the biggest hug and rubbed my back just like a comforting momma would.

I didn't see Cassie right away; I think she was hiding.

Once I saw her across the room, I immediately went to her. She couldn't even look me in the eyes. I knew she felt the weight of the world on her shoulders in guilt.

"I want to talk to you. . . in private," I said.

Without looking up, she nodded. "We can go into Easton's room," she mumbled.

I could tell she was medicated, too; her words came out slow, and she seemed out of it.

We went down the hall to Easton's room. I didn't shut the door, as I didn't want her to feel any more uncomfortable or scared than she already was.

I grabbed both her hands and held them tight. I was trying to make eye contact with her, but she was avoiding it. "Cassie, I need to tell you that Cody and I don't blame you. This was a tragic accident. . . I am not mad at you. If anything, I feel closer to you in some weird way. Like we're bonded for life in this horrible way. I love you."

I told her about Pastor Jim coming to my house at the exact time I needed him most.

We talked about God and our faith. I knew that was the only thing that would get us through this.

I encouraged her to read the Bible and pray, pray, pray.

She shared with me that Pastor Jim had called her. She had never met him before, either, but he'd called her after the accident when she truly needed it most, as well. She was at her weakest moment, curled up on the floor crying when the phone rang. We knew God was working through Jim to send us some hope and comfort.

We talked about our sons being in the car during the accident.

"Do you think they saw anything?" I asked.

"I really don't know."

We don't know what kept them in the car. We figured they were in their almost an hour before the fire department got them out of the vehicle. Both boys could easily unbuckle their seat belts and get out if they wanted to.

"Thank God they didn't get out!" I said. That would've been a horrific sight for them to see. "Wyatt told me Easton was crying and asking where you were. He said he was scared. Wyatt told him the firetrucks were there to kill a giant spider in the driveway," I told her.

"Really? Weird. Easton just said he was scared and didn't know where I went."

We discussed the morning of the accident over and over. I reassured her there was nothing she could have done.

If anything, this was my fault. I was so consumed with Wyatt's fit that I wasn't paying attention. I should have known exactly where Rowyn was.

Why was I not holding her? I was always holding her, so why wasn't I holding her then?

I was angry at myself and at the situation, but I was trying so hard to stay strong and hold it together in front of Cassie.

Somehow, I had the strength. I knew it was God. . . and Rowyn giving it to me.

AFTER WE GOT HOME that afternoon, cousins Nikki and Robin wanted to talk to Cody and I about planning Rowyn's funeral and celebration of life.

I knew they had wholeheartedly started planning arrangements, and I was so thankful I didn't have to do it. I honestly had no idea how to or what to even do.

"Brynn, can we talk to you for a minute? We want to go over some of the ideas we have with you," Robin asked.

I honestly had no energy to plan anything but knew it had to be done. I wanted the last party we were planning for Rowyn to be nothing but the best. They had already made phone calls for nearly everything. I was so overwhelmed with what they were asking me; I couldn't believe how much they already accomplished in a few days.

We discussed venue. We needed somewhere large enough for our family and then some. We had no idea planning then that over five hundred people would show up to Rowyn's celebration of life.

"The Riverbend Ranch has offered to donate their space for you," Robin said.

I loved the facility. The more I thought about it, I couldn't picture a better venue. It was rustic, country, close to home, close to the burial site, and special considering it was where we took the kids to pick out Rowyn's first and only Christmas tree.

We were actually at the venue for a friend's wedding the summer before with Rowyn. I remember getting her all dressed up in a special Juicy Couture dress and a matching big flower headband for the occasion. It was an easy decision to make.

Not only was it meaningful to me, it was also being generously donated to us. "Okay, so we have called a few flower shops, and we have a few people reaching out who want to donate services for that, as well. We just need to know what you want."

I knew what I wanted for that. I wanted everything to represent exactly what Rowyn's personality was. "Gerbera daisies. . . I always had daisies and wildflowers for her and she loved them," I said.

They were her signature flower. I could picture her clearly helping me water my flower pots on the front porch just a few days prior, sniffing the daisies and giggling.

I also had them at her first birthday party for décor all over the house. They always reminded me of her—wild, bright and cheery—so it was an easy decision for me to make.

I wanted different shades of coral and pink Gerbera daisies for Rowyn. The girls already had a friend making a slideshow of Rowyn's life to show at the celebration of life, as well as extra copies for the family.

They had started designing the programs for the funeral. I was blown away with the amount of work that had gone into planning already.

"We wanted to do something special and memorable. How do you feel about a balloon release after the ceremony?" they asked.

I thought it was a beautiful idea, like we were sending them up to Heaven for her, and guests could write messages on the balloons if they wanted to.

I loved all the ideas so far. I reached for my wallet to see how much money I had in there. I pulled out everything I'd made from the week before.

On top of the cash was a check, the only check in my wallet, and it was from Cassie Miller.

She was one of the last clients I'd handled before the accident.

How ironic.

"So, how much is all of this going to cost?" I asked.

"We really don't want you to worry about that right now. Just know that Cousin Jen has started a GoFundMe account for you guys and support is pouring in. I don't think you need to worry about paying for anything at this point."

What a relief that was. I had no idea. I was so out of it the last few days I didn't even know what had taken place. Nikki and Robin reassured me that whatever needed to be paid for upfront would be taken care of, and we could worry about the finances later.

That in itself was a huge relief. I knew it was going to be pretty costly but had no idea on even an estimated cost. I stared at Cassie's check. *There is no way I can deposit this.* I tore up her check and threw it away.

There was so much more to discuss. Music, colors, décor, a pastor, designing the pamphlets, food, dates. . . and then some more.

It was a lot to think about. "I honestly trust your judgement on these things 100%. What you have done so far has been perfect," I told them. "I just want it to be meaningful and special in every way possible."

I knew Nikki and Robin would put their whole hearts into making all the arrangements for the dreaded day, and I was so thankful that I could trust them with the decisions. I was having a hard enough time making even simple daily decisions, let alone big ones that would be reflecting my daughter's short life. I trusted them completely to make the day the best it could possibly be.

THAT NIGHT, SHERI CAME into my closet where I had been hiding, needing to talk to me about a few things. The horrible things you never ever think you'll have to think about.

"So, I talked to the funeral home today," she said.

I didn't really want to know what they had to say, but I knew it was something I needed to hear.

"They have completed her autopsy. . . and they want you to pick out what you want her to be buried in."

I could tell Sherie didn't want to be talking about it just as much as I didn't. I knew she was strong enough that she was going to be my strength, though.

I blankly looked at her confused. I didn't think about it before, I guess. "What do you mean they finished her autopsy?" I asked.

I couldn't believe that after all the trauma her little body had already been through they were going to cut her open and examine her. I wanted to throw up and started trembling. I wasn't prepared for that.

My mind flooded with visions of my lifeless, naked baby laid out on a metal examining table, being cut open.

"Oh, my God, I can't handle this! You're telling me they had to cut her open!" I yelled.

My sadness quickly was turning into anger. I was so disgusted by the thoughts and images playing in my mind.

Sheri was trying to calm me down. I knew it wasn't her fault, but I knew she was the only one strong enough in my family to be my punching bag.

"I want to see her!" I demanded.

Sheri looked at me in shock and just started shaking her head. She slowly hung her head down, and I could tell there was more she didn't want to tell me.

"What? What is it? I want to see her one last time! If it was your baby, wouldn't you want to see them one last time before they went into the ground?" I yelled.

She looked up at me, her eyes brimming with tears, and continued to shake her head no. "They don't recommend that you see her, Brynn."

I didn't understand. . . I was getting so furious.

"Why?" I screamed. "Is her face really bad? Did they cut her face? I just want to hold her little chubby hands one last time. I know she won't be the same or look the same! I've already seen her dead. Held her dead! Kissed her cold little hands! What is going to be worse than that? Why can't I see her now?" My anger was turning into downright rage, and Sheri was taking it all.

Without realizing it, I was yelling at her like it was her fault. I just couldn't understand how another mother didn't appreciate where I was coming from.

It would be my last and only chance to see my baby before she went into the ground. *Nobody should tell me I can't see my daughter! She was my baby and if they cut her up, I'm going to fly off the handle.*

I raged on while Sheri continued to take it. She stood her ground and still insisted that I didn't see Rowyn. I was angry at *her*.

I screamed until I broke.

I sobbed until I crumbled.

Sheri reached out to grab me and held me. "I'm so sorry, I just don't want you to see her like that. She's not going to look the same," she whispered as she held me.

This I knew, but I wasn't ready to make up my mind about it. It was a decision I wanted to talk about with Cody, and I needed a day or two to think about it. Sheri held me and rubbed my back as we both cried. She knew as much as I did that I needed to think about it.

THAT NIGHT, CODY AND I laid in bed in silence, staring at the ceiling. I had kept the bedside lamp on for a little hope that the Devil wouldn't dare show himself to me in the light.

I looked over at Cody, and he had tears streaming down his face. The tears were pooling into his ears. I also had tears rolling down my face, but I was trying to fight back the noises that came along with them.

I was trying to be strong for him. I knew he could snap at any moment, too.

"Honey, we really need to make a pact that we will always be here for each other through this. There's no way we can do it without one another."

He nodded, still avoiding eye contact, staring off blankly as he swallowed a big lump in his throat.

I reached for his hands that were folded on his stomach, squeezing them. "Can I pray aloud?" I asked.

Cody turned onto his side and finally looked into my eyes then nodded again.

As we held hands and both continued to cry, I prayed. I didn't even know what to pray about. Just to be able to live through this tragedy.

I prayed for reassurance that my daughter was okay up in Heaven in the arms of God, to comfort us in our time of need and my family.

I was begging in my prayer for anything God could give us that would provide some sort of hope or strength.

When I finished praying, I opened my eyes. I looked into the eyes of my husband and I could see how broken he was.

He was lost, the same as I. He didn't have to say anything; I could see the pain all over his face.

Cody got up and walked to the bathroom. I continued to watch him, like I was watching just in case I needed to protect him from that damn Devil lurking around.

Instead of going into the separate bathroom area, Cody stepped into the large soaking tub, which I could still see from my bed.

I could see his silhouette as he stood in the tub and stared out the large windows looking into the fields. I remembered the gun I had sitting right next to him. It was on top of the vanity out of the reach of the kids, but I had stored my pistol away there for some time. It was within his reach. The terrible fear took over me.

*This is it. . . my husband's going to kill himself now.*

I laid there terrified. I didn't know what to say. I continued staring at him, waiting for him to reach up on top of the vanity and grab the gun. It seemed like forever that he was in there.

I could still see him just standing there, but he wasn't doing anything other than staring out the window.

*If I see him reach for the gun, then I will start screaming. . . Then everybody will come running upstairs and help me wrestle the gun away from him.*

I had the scenario played out in my head just in case. I knew how he was feeling, but I knew 150% that I could not live without him, too.

I needed him.

Our son needed his daddy and I needed my husband.

Finally, after he spent a long time by himself in the bathroom just staring out the window, he walked back into the bedroom and crawled into bed.

I had a huge pit in my stomach but felt like I could breathe again. I was so anxious I had been holding my breath.

I was exhausted and felt like every minute was taking hours to pass.

All I wanted to do was sleep.

Every time I would close my eyes and attempt to sleep, all I could see was images of my deceased daughter. Horrible images would replay in my mind.

Things worse than what happened even started creeping into my imagination. I was in a nightmare but awake through all of it. I was terrified to close my eyes.

I started reading my Bible for any bit of comfort I could find. I knew the only thing that could beat the attacks of the Devil on me would be God himself. I was not strong enough to make it on my own and I knew it. I was trying so hard to keep myself together somewhat to comfort my husband.

I definitely wasn't going to tell him that I was terrified the Devil had crept into our home and was going to strike again at any minute. He would think I was crazy.

I was going crazy.

I felt completely out of control and helpless, no longer even able to control my own thoughts.

THAT NIGHT WAS ONE of the longest of my life. I watched the sun come up through the windows that just a few hours before I saw my husband standing in front of, I think contemplating suicide.

I laid there and the tears started flowing. They gradually got more and more difficult to keep quiet.

I didn't want to wake Cody, as I knew he had been awake most of the night.

As I got out of bed, I could hear some movement downstairs.

I walked downstairs and into the living room where Randy and Sheri had been sleeping.

"Are you all right?" Randy asked as he sat up quickly from the couch.

He was probably up all night, too.

I shook my head and walked toward him. He hugged me tight as we sat on the couch together.

Once he hugged me, I lost it even more. It was like he was giving me permission to be weak. He held me and cried, too. I needed to tell him about the gun.

I was scared to even touch it myself. I felt so reckless that I shouldn't even be near anything dangerous. Through my sobs, I told Randy about the gun. I started crying even harder.

"I'm so scared of what Cody might do." I told him. I was so distraught that I couldn't even make sense of my own words anymore, but he knew what I was asking of him.

He continued to hug me tight and reassured me that he would get the gun and put it away in the safe and not to worry about it. I felt safe with him. I knew he would get us through this and not leave our sides. He was my strength and comfort I needed then the most.

# Chapter Fifteen

## CASSIE

### THE SECOND WORST DAY OF MY LIFE

*"In hard times, she had learned three things: She was stronger than she ever imagined, Jesus was closer than she ever realized and she was loved more than she ever knew."*
*Author Unknown*

It was here, that dreadful Monday and day of the services.

My girlfriends had all planned to be at my house that morning to help me get ready for the day. They knew how difficult it would be to put the ugly dress on or do anything for that matter.

I was sitting on a small stepstool in the bathroom, shedding tears and filled with anxiety as Jen straight-ironed my hair.

As she stood above me, steam rolling from the iron, my phone rang. I was a bit startled as I didn't know who would be calling me, but it was a 264 number. That meant Tenino, and immediately I thought it was the police.

My fears for the following days were that the police department would be calling to let me know there were some charges.

I answered, and to my surprise it wasn't the police. It was a man named Jim. A man who I now call my pastor.

He had connected with Brynn and Cody, and had been given my information. He was doing the services that day, and wanted to call and pray with me beforehand.

I started bawling, letting him pray with me on the phone, desperately wanting him to make it all go away and help me somehow. It was a short conversation, but he offered as much support as he could. And I couldn't help but think it was the perfect time to have received that phone call.

As I sat there, I let the girls continue to do their work on me, but really nothing could help. I didn't care; I just wanted to get it all over with.

When it was time to leave, my mom went to Wanda's house for coffee to wait for us during the burial ceremony.

My husband and I rode with Ron and Jen as I hysterically bawled the entire way from Grand Mound to Tenino.

As hard as that ride was for me, I could only imagine how Brynn and Cody must have felt.

During the drive, Aaron held me close and kept his hand tight on mine, giving me the support I needed at the time.

I had tissues stuffed in every corner from friends. When we pulled up to the cemetery, it became real for me.

This whole thing—the agonizing last week of life—had come to this. It was time to lay Rowyn to rest.

Almost all of the guests were already there, except for Brynn and Cody and their closest family members who were arriving in a limo.

As we began to walk through the dead grass of the cemetery on that overcast and gloomy day, I could barely stand up to walk. I could not contain the volume of my excessive crying, it was just loud. Reality was finally hitting, walking up to this tiny casket, a tent, and her grieving family.

At one point, I dropped a wad of tissues and I think my husband thought I was falling to the ground. As if it could have been any more awkward and horrendous than it already was.

When we made our way to the tent, I continued to cry, unable to keep it together.

I was approached by Cody's Uncle Rob, who was at the scene the day of the accident.

He hugged me tight and said to me, "I know you are hurting, but today is about them."

I knew exactly what he was saying. I never wanted it to be about me, ever. I didn't want the eyes to glance at me as I walked up, but I was the driver. How could they not? It was like being the elephant in the room; I couldn't help but stick out in the crowd.

It was only minutes of standing off to the side when I saw the limo pull up. I watched as Brynn and Cody got out. I could only imagine what that would be like arriving at their own daughter's funeral. Another reminder of how wrong this whole situation was. *We should be at work, doing normal things like we were a week ago. Instead, we are at their daughter's funeral.*

The song "In the Arms of an Angel," was sung by Rowyn's Aunt Emily, which was unbearable to hear. Brynn had told me just days before the accident at my hair appointment how close Rowyn and Wyatt were to Braiden and Emily. How she held it together during that song is beyond me. I know she was hurting. As were the family members who spoke, and those who were just too beside themselves with grief to speak. In my mind, I felt like such a killer. Such a horrible, no-good, unworthy person. I was ashamed of everything about myself, and I really did not know how I was standing there. But I did it. Because I had to.

Cody's cousin Nikki came around with Gerbera daisies to be laid on Rowyn's casket. She made sure to pull the biggest one from her bundle to give to me.

Walking in that line up in front of her closest family to put the daisy down was so difficult. There are not words to describe facing a situation like that; it was just awful and something you would not wish on anyone in the world.

I turned back to give Cody and Brynn a hug. I whispered to Brynn, "I am just so sorry."

I don't know how many times a person could really say that, but to this day, I feel like I need to say it. I don't, though, because I know they know.

When we loaded up in the truck, a big relief was off my shoulders. The harder of the two events was over.

We went back to Momma Wanda's house for some coffee. I needed to fix myself up, as I looked as good as I felt.

It was then that we headed to Jensen's Barn for the celebration of life which was overflowing with people. Pulling into another unique situation, my anxiety was out of control.

There were so many people there that groups of people were outside who could not get all the way in the barn. Walking in with my friends and my mom beside me, I kept my sunglasses on and put the bravest face on I had.

Having still been considered new to this town of Tenino, I wasn't sure what to think. Being a small town, there are still tons of people I do not know.

But after this accident, there are tons of people who know me. It is not the way you would like to become known in a small town, but lucky for me they embraced me.

The first thing I saw off to my left was a table with a lot of photos and items of Rowyn.

It was just enough to knock the living shit out of me. My heart was pounding out of my chest, the tears fell all over again, and I think I could have fallen to the ground right then and there. People were just embracing me from every direction, some I knew, some were introducing themselves, and some didn't say anything but just hugged me.

Since the accident, I hadn't been able to look at any photographs of Rowyn. Brynn would text me how much it helped her because the final visions of her were not good or how she should be remembered. I just couldn't, though; it was more painful for me to see the beautiful life I snatched away.

Seeing all of these gorgeous pictures of Rowyn was heartbreaking. My in-laws found me, as did some other friends who had come. We scurried off toward the left side of the barn, out of the way and for me, I'd hoped out of sight.

The slide show of Rowyn began to play and as awful as it is for me to say, it was pure torture. It was like someone was taking a knife and digging it into the wounds I had as hard as they could.

Watching the little video clips of her just days before she died. Seeing her wander through a field being filmed and she had no idea, just a couple weeks prior to the accident. It was all too much to bear.

Finally, it was time for the balloon release, which was hard. To see her whole family and closest friends in a large group in the center, grieving together and releasing her balloons.

I have never felt so small in my entire life. I wanted to die that day.

As soon as that part was over, we skipped the food and got out of there. We came back to our house, and many of our friends did, too. It had been a long week for all of us.

My in-laws brought pizza for us all, and I put sweats on and lay on my couch. It felt like a million bricks had been lifted off my shoulders once that day was over.

But it left me still with a remaining question.

*What do I do now?*

# Chapter Sixteen

## BRYNN

### THIS CAN'T REALLY BE HAPPENING

*"But those who trust in the Lord will find new strength. They will soar high on wings like eagles. They will run and not grow weary. They will walk and not faint."*
*Isaiah 40:31*

I could hardly see through my tears. I was in my closet, alone, trying to comprehend what was happening. In front of me, I had laid out the outfit that I had picked for Rowyn to be buried in. She had actually picked it out the day before she passed away. That day will always be etched into my memory. It was so special, like God gave me that last day with her to spend quality time together. She hadn't been feeling well so I made a doctor appointment for her that Monday morning. I would rarely get a sitter for Wyatt, but since Rowyn wasn't feeling well, I sent him to Randy and Sheri's house. Rowyn and I had the day to ourselves. I took her to the doctor that morning and I will never forget her chubby little hands pressed against the glass of the fish tank in the waiting room. She was fascinated by the fish. She would stare at them and then look over at me to make sure I was watching too.

Even though she wasn't feeling well her mood would never show it; she was happy and content. While at the doctor's office, our nurse that day was actually one of my childhood friends. We had grown up from second grade through high school together and still remained in touch after all those years. It was a blessing to see her and share my beautiful daughter with her. I now know that God wanted her to meet Rowyn before she left. After leaving the doctor's office with the diagnosis being a simple cold, I decided to take her shopping.

We never got to go just the two of us girls. Even though Rowyn was so young, she already loved clothes and had her own sense of style. I took her to Carters and let her run free in the store. I wanted her to enjoy our time shopping together. I had picked out this teal zip-up hooded sweatshirt with matching pants and showed it to her. "Look, sissy, do you like this?" I asked her.

She looked at it briefly and quickly grabbed the coral pink version sitting on the display next to it.

I laughed. "Okay, we will get the pink one." She already had such an opinion of what she liked and didn't like.

I also picked out a few new shirts, as well as vacation clothes for our upcoming trip to Mexico. We enjoyed our time there together so much. It was something silly that was important to me. I always had told Cody he best get a raise so I could take our little girl shopping and spoil her. It was fun for me to have that moment with her.

NOW THAT CORAL PINK sweat suit was laid out on my floor in the closet.

Rowyn never got to wear it. I choose it for her to be buried in because she had just picked it out herself just days before on our last day together. She had so many beautiful dresses that I could have chosen to lay her to rest in, but I hated the idea of her being uncomfortable and cold. All I wanted was her to be warm and cozy. I pictured her tiny little body in her casket. The chilling image made my tears stream down my cheeks heavier than before.

I hated it!

*I can't believe I am doing this right now, laying out my daughter's clothes for her funeral. It's disgusting.*

I also decided to put her in a shirt that we had bought that day as well. It had a cupcake on it, with the word "Sweet" across the chest, just like her. I would give anything just to hold her right now. I hated everything about what I was doing, but I wanted what she wore to be special and meaningful. I chose her brother's hand me down Converse sneakers that she loved. I wanted a piece of her brother with her at all times. They were rugged and worn, but she loved wearing them. One by one, I glued tiny crystal gems onto the toe of the navy blue Converse sneakers. My hands were quivering and I could hardly see through my tears but I wanted them to be perfect for her. I then set aside her oversized hot-pink bow for her hair that she wore all the time. She hated it when her crazy wild curls would get in her face, so I would always clip them back with a bow.

"Brynn, can I come in?" Sheri peeked her head around the corner of the doorway.

Unable to speak, I nodded for her to come in. I gulped, trying to contain my emotions. She came in and sat down cross-legged with me, trying to act as normal as possible while watching me glue gems onto my daughter's sneakers. I didn't know what to say. I just sat quietly, still trying to pick up stones one by one with my shaky hands. "I just want her to be warm enough. . . and comfortable," I said. My voice cracked and I started to cry again. "I hate this! I just picture her in that little casket and I don't want her to feel smothered in there."

My tears manifested into sobs. Sheri comforted me and started rubbing my back. She didn't know what to say. What do you tell a mother who is preparing for her one-year-old daughter's burial? There was nothing she could say to make me feel better.

THE PIT IN MY STOMACH felt big enough to swallow me whole.

Again, I sat in my closet trying to hide from the world and my pain. Having not slept in the last week, and hardly eaten, I was sleep-deprived, weak, and frail.

Sitting cross-legged, I stared hopelessly up at the long, hot pink maxi dress I had chosen to wear for my baby's funeral. It was such a beautiful dress and a shame I would never want to wear it again.

I chose to wear color for her special day because she was such a bright, happy, young soul, and black wouldn't have been suitable for her. She didn't even own anything black in her entire wardrobe.

As I sat there, feeling like I never wanted to get up, I had no idea what day of the week it was, or even the month. I was so out of sorts I just knew it was the dreaded day of Rowyn's burial and celebration of life.

I heard the bedroom door open slowly, and I waited quietly to see who it was. I stayed in my closet and in came Aunt Cindy with a plate of food of pretty much anything I could ever want.

"Here, I made you a plate." Cindy practically begged me to eat. "Won't you please eat a little something today? Just anything in your tummy will help."

I most definitely didn't have an appetite but reached up for the plate. "Thank you. . . I will eat something," I said, just to appease her.

Standing, I peered into my bedroom. The group of girls was in there, I think giving me my privacy of the closet, but close enough to be there if I needed them.

Cousins Nikki and Robin walked in with tears in their eyes. I could tell they had been crying but they were trying to be strong for me. They both looked beautiful and already put together for the dreaded day.

"We are going to head out to finish decorating. . . and make sure everything is just perfect," Nikki said.

"We don't want you to worry about anything. It looks beautiful already," Robin reassured me.

I knew it would be perfect. That was all they had been focusing on was putting together the most special day as possible.

I didn't know what to say, because how could I thank them?

"Thank you. . . I love you girls so much," I uttered, hugging them each as tightly as I could, even though I felt so weak.

I knew I didn't need to worry about it being anything but perfect for my baby.

I stared at my reflection in my bathroom mirror as I got ready. I hardly recognized myself.

The pale, frail, weak girl in the mirror was not who I was used to seeing. I was defeated, and I looked every bit of it. As the tears rolled down my cheeks, I would wipe my face and start over again.

My sense of how much time had passed was gone. My family and closest girlfriends surrounded me in my bathroom in my attempt to get ready. I knew they were partially there to keep me on task as well as for support.

After what seemed like an eternity of getting ready, I knew it was as good as I was going to get. I felt like hell and didn't really care anymore what I looked like. The only thing I cared about was my dress reflecting how I felt about my daughter.

I looked out the front windows to see a police car and a limo out in my roundabout driveway. The same driveway Rowyn was just lying in a few days before. A flashback of Rowyn's delicate little body face-down in her turquoise polka dot pajamas consumed my thoughts. I couldn't focus on what was actually outside. She was all I could envision.

I took a couple deep breaths and leaned against the wall to keep myself from wilting to the ground. I closed my eyes for a few seconds and reopened them, hoping the horrific image would be gone.

It wasn't. . . I took another deep breath.

I turned away from the window and looked behind me. There was my entire family just waiting for me, waiting for me to be ready to walk out the door. I didn't want to be, but I knew it was time. We all walked outside together.

As we headed down the sidewalk toward the driveway, I saw Cody make eye contact with the local police officer who was sitting in his car.

He nodded at him, as if saying an unspoken thank you. He was there to watch over our home while we were away at the services.

The department had arranged for an officer to be there at all times throughout the day.

We continued on to the limo. The young man greeted us so politely and opened the door for us.

"Thank you so much," I said. I had not met him before nor did I know who he was, but his family had contacted us and donated their limo services for the day.

As my family piled into the limo, I stayed outside for a moment to talk to him. He shared that his family had also lost a child, and it was dear to his mother's heart that they reached out to us.

After our brief conversation, we ended with a quick hug and I got into the limo. I sat closest to the door, and my immediate family surrounded me.

Wyatt thought it was so special to be riding in such a fancy car. With his excitement, it was obvious he did not understand we were going to his sister's funeral.

This was the first death he had ever experienced, and he was not old enough to understand. How could a child even begin to comprehend something like this?

We pulled into the cemetery and cars lined the gravel road leading up to the gravesite we had chosen.

Our friends and family had taken over the small-town cemetery.

I was trembling and my teeth started chattering. I could not believe what was happening or that this was my reality. I wanted to hide in the limo and never get out.

The pit in my stomach was growing by the second, and I was so nauseated and dizzy. Our driver opened the door for us, and I knew I had to get out. I slid toward the door and exited the car. I was weak in the knees and held onto the driver for stability.

I waited for everyone else to get out of the car and linked arms with Cody. I couldn't speak, nor did I have anything to say.

He seemed much stronger than I, and I could not understand how he seemed so calm. I wanted to shrivel up and die.

We were the last to walk over to the graveside. Pastor Jim was standing next to the casket and hugged us both as we approached.

I avoided eye contact with everyone. I couldn't handle it. I knew I would lose it as soon as I made eye contact with anybody.

We were seated in the front row just a few feet away from the grave. Rowyn's little white casket was closed. We had it adorned with an oversized turquoise Tiffany's bow on top, just like her bedroom décor. Multiple shades of coral and pink Gerbera daisies were arranged all over, as well.

*This can't be happening. Not to us.*

As I stared in disbelief at the scene in front of me, my trembling quickly turned into a severe shaking that took over my entire body. I had to sit down. I didn't think I could stand much longer; I felt like I could collapse to the ground at any moment.

Pastor Jim began to speak. His heartfelt emotion poured out of him as well as his passion for God. I could not focus on what he was saying, but I knew it was meaningful and beautiful in every way. Jim shared aloud a very personal letter I had written to Rowyn.

*To our sweet sweet Angel Rowyn,*
*There are not enough words to even express how much we love you! We love your heart, kindness, laughter, charisma, curiosity, your adventurous nature, spirit, your little bubble belly, and tiny little butt.*
*Your sparkling blue eyes, curly blonde hair, and perfect little smile warm our hearts.*
*Your spitfire attitude makes us laugh.*
*You truly are the most amazing and beautiful soul we have ever met, and we are honored to have called you ours.*

*We cherish every second we spent with you.*
*You are the light of our lives.*
*We will cherish every memory we have from the minute our*
*eyes connected for the first time to the last time we got to hold*
*you.*
*There are so many things we looked forward to doing with*
*you one day that we never got to do. Mommy couldn't wait to*
*take you on shopping sprees and spend too much money,*
*paint our toes, do your hair for prom one day, show your first*
*boyfriend embarrassing photos, have our first cocktail*
*together, take you on vacation, live and laugh with you.*
*You are my best friend, and I planned on it always being that*
*way.*
*Your daddy couldn't wait to take you hunting, to teach you to*
*drive, shoot a bow, ride a bike, buy your first pink gun, and*
*walk you down the aisle...and Daddy thanks you for sticking*
*around for him to have that chance to walk you down the*
*aisle at Braiden and Emily's wedding and stand at the altar*
*with him; it meant the world to him.*
*We thank you for all the hugs, kisses, pats on the back, laughs,*
*love, and butt bombs. We will never forget the sound of your*
*voice calling us, the sound of your laugh, the sound of your*
*feet running across the floor, the smell of your baby shampoo,*
*the sound of shooting your pistols in the air, and chomping*
*berries.*
*You made us better people and softened our hearts, humbled*
*us and brought us closer to God and closer together.*
*Please watch over Mommy, Daddy, and Wyatt. Please come*
*to visit when you can. We will be waiting to feel the wind and*
*see the pink sky.*

*Drop it like it's hot in Heaven! We cherish you always.*
*Love,*
*Mommy & Daddy*

The moment he finished, I could hear the cries and the sobbing coming from all around me. I let out a painful wail myself.

It hurt! It hurt *so* badly, in a way that I had never experienced pain.

I was lost, dead inside, and numb all at the same time. All I could think was that I wanted to open up her casket and hold her one last time. Images were flashing in my mind of what Rowyn would look like inside there. The control freak in me wanted to know if she looked the way I wanted her to.

*Is her hair styled the way I asked them to?*

*Does she have enough room in there with all of her special belongings without being smothered?*

*Does she look like herself?*

*Was she mutilated after her autopsy?*

*I will never know because I did not take the opportunity to see her. I just had to believe that she was the way I wanted her to be.*

I was going to have a full-on breakdown, right there in front of everyone.

The only thing keeping me from imploding was my son sitting a few seats away. I could not let him see me go off the deep end like I was contemplating. He had already witnessed more than any little boy should ever have to, and I decided there was no way I would make this moment even more traumatic for him.

After our intimate graveside ceremony, we attended Rowyn's celebration of life, located just a mile down the country road at beautiful Riverbend Ranch.

The venue was breathtaking. The owners, being longtime local residents and family friends, donated the facility. More than 500 guests attended that day, more people than the venue had ever seen. I had never felt or seen a community come together like I witnessed that day. It was truly amazing, beautiful and humbling to experience such support and love from so many.

# Chapter Seventeen

CASSIE

UNBEARABLE PAIN, YET LOVE

*"Grief never ends…But it changes. It's a passage, not a place to stay. Grief is not a sign of weakness, nor a lack of faith…It is the price of love."*
*Author Unknown*

The days and weeks following the burial can only be described as unimaginable. Trying to pick the pieces up from my ordinary life felt impossible.

My mom had to get back to her life at that point, which consisted of working in the day and caring for my terminally ill grandmother by night. When she left and made the four-hour trek back across the state, reality set in a little further.

We had a nanny working for us for about two and a half weeks by that point, which had to have been provided by the grace of God, because I do not know what I would have done without her. She arrived every morning as scheduled, and while I locked myself in my room to cry, sleep and read anything self-help I could get my hands on, she cared for my kids.

When her shift ended, Aaron would be home. It wasn't that I couldn't be alone with my kids, but just about every little thing was too overwhelming for me to handle. So as yucky as it sounds to say, I really didn't spend time alone with them for a while.

My therapist had me do some EMDR (Eye Movement Desensitization and Reprocessing) therapy in attempts to get myself driving again. It was a technique used a lot of times in cases of trauma and described to me as a way of taking some of the emotion out of the difficult memory.

I actually thought this seemed very strange during my therapy session, and I could not really understand how it would help me.

But oddly enough, it did.

I would be lying if I said I don't struggle with anxiety, flashbacks and stress while driving now, but I am capable. Being able to drive was very important for me because without that ability, I would have been relying on anyone and everyone to help me survive.

During that time, I was in therapy two days a week and my son was still in preschool two days a week.

I would take him to preschool and drop him off. I'd drive past that same driveway as the day of the accident.

Going to the same preschool we never made it to that dreadful day, and I would see my grief-stricken friend arrive with her one child instead of two, looking as lost and sad as I felt.

I would generally leave preschool and head to therapy. My new routine was becoming as unordinary as it sounded. I spent a lot of time sitting in Starbucks with a heavy stack of books I carried alongside me. I would lug around a Bible, a journal, and two separate devotionals, Solo and Jesus Calling. I would read, highlight, take notes, and search everywhere for some sign from God.

When I would return to school to pick Easton up, a lot of times Brynn and I would be parked there early together. She would often stroll over to my car where we would sit, and I would cry.

She said to me once, "I am so sorry that it is so hard for you to see me."

It was one of the kindest things I could have ever expected to hear from her. I was thinking how awful it must have been for her to see me. It was difficult to explain what grief looked like, because everyone wore it differently. And Brynn and I were perfect examples of that statement, both trying to cope and heal in different ways, but strangely, coming together in the same. We were both grieving, just in our own ways.

Brynn managed to gracefully keep herself together during all of these days we would see one another in those first weeks following the accident.

I, on the other hand, was never so graceful.

I was lucky to have showered, and wearing makeup was something I struggled with, too. It was so unimportant to me at that point. I guess you could say that how crappy I looked fully reflected how crappy that I felt.

It didn't feel okay to try to look good. It felt wrong.

*This whole situation is wrong. Who am I and how did I get myself into this situation?*

Each week, Tuesday rolled around. It was a struggle, to say the least. The day of the week that everything in our family's worlds changed forever.

I had been in contact with my boss during this whole time.

When would I return to work, and what would it be like?

What would I be capable of doing there?

I was a supervisor of unit 5 in the Office of Disability Determination Services. I oversaw a staff of eight, two of whom were trainees. It was so important to me to get back to that job. I had worked so hard for it. I started in an entry-level position just five and a half years earlier.

I had decided I could be a career-driven woman as well as a devoted mom.

Why couldn't I have both?

The reality hit me when I tried to return to work three days a week in October. I was sitting in my office on my second day back when I suffered my very first panic attack. I was working off my normal three computer screens and every piece of work that I had pulled up to work on that morning felt impossible.

I kept telling myself, "I'll get to that later."

And then it happened.

I struggled to breathe. I choked to get air. I bent over in my chair in pure shock. *What is happening to me?*

The more I tried to gain control of my breath, the more intense it got. My hands began to go numb and clinch just as they had that day at the scene. A coworker walked by and went to get my boss. I was comforted in my office for a while, and finally was walked to my car by my boss Leann, a psychologist from work, and my coworker friend Amy.

Together, they helped me through the horror of what I had just experienced. They drove me home, got me into bed, and then left for me to sleep.

It was a day I will never forget. A self-realization that I was broken in more ways than I even realized at that point. I could not go back; it was just too soon.

As I worked my way through the rest of October, the dreaded first holiday approached quickly, Halloween.

I remembered Rowyn just the year before, in her fish costume.

How could I go out trick-or-treating with my boys when I couldn't even walk down a Halloween aisle in a store because of the gore and fake blood everywhere?

I would never see Halloween the way I used to.

It was one of those Tuesdays or Thursdays in late October when I was picking up Easton from school. Brynn was there picking up Wyatt, and she wandered over to my car where we sat and talked. How lost we were, how broken we felt, and ultimately how sad and sorry we were.

"I feel like I need to be doing something to honor my daughter," she said. "I feel like I need to be starting a charity for her or something."

What Brynn didn't know was that after the accident, my mom had suggested we do a Run for Rowyn in her honor each year.

We were reached out to by the Adam Craig Foundation just days after, wanting to raise money for my family and me, but instead I asked for future help with getting the run together.

I knew this was the right time to bring it up to her, and so I did. I told her of the idea to do the run, and she asked me, "Where would the money go?"

"We could do a scholarship fund in her name each year or whatever you think?" I suggested.

When we left that day, it would be a little while before I saw Brynn again. I had decided to leave to go to the Tri Cities to be near my family for a week.

To my surprise, I received a text message from her the very next day saying she had discussed it with Cody, and that she really wanted to move forward with it. She had so many ideas coming to her that she suggested it be more than just a run. She decided to name it Raise for Rowyn. It was absolutely perfect, and yet we had no clue what we were about to do with it.

# Chapter Eighteen

### BRYNN

#### LIVING FOR SIGNS FROM ABOVE

*"I have made you and I will carry you. I will sustain you and I will rescue you."*
*Isaiah 46:4*

The next few weeks there was a heavy fog over me and my home. I didn't know what day it was or month still.

I kept asking my family over and over again, but every time they would tell me the answer, it was like I was hearing it for the first time.

My every sense of reality had left me.

I found it hard to even read text messages on my phone.

My mind was so boggled I would stare at a message and try to read it, but I just couldn't seem to make sense of it. I would get completely overwhelmed with the simplest task; even taking a shower had become something that was exhausting to me. My drive was gone.

I began spending my days looking for any sign that could be from Rowyn. I would wake up every morning and ask, "Tell Mommy somehow or some way that you're with me."

When I opened my eyes many mornings, I would see the pink sky from my bedroom with the sun coming up. I could feel her presence and know she was there.

Some mornings, I would wake up and still hear her sweet little voice saying, "Mom, Mom."

I would replay it in my mind every day, as if I couldn't let that morning ritual go.

She was my early bird, always waking me up with the sunrise. That began to be my hardest time of the day, but also the closest I could feel her presence.

Another sign I began getting almost daily was a visit from a Red-tailed hawk.

This would happen at the time of day I needed it most, or in the most random locations. I would always see a hawk on many occasions while at the cemetery visiting Rowyn. If I didn't see one there, it seemed to be sitting on a fencepost on my drive home or flying above the car.

This became symbolic to me because during Rowyn's Celebration of Life, I was standing outside in a trance after the balloon release in honor of her and someone told me a hawk circled above me.

At the time, I was too out of it to think that it could be a sign, but as time passed, I was positive Rowyn showed her presence that day.

On my worst days, I could be just climbing out of bed and a Red-tailed hawk would fly by my window at the exact moment I looked out.

I decided it wasn't a coincidence; it would happen too frequently, and I would always get this feeling that it was a sign from above.

On another occasion, my husband was driving down the freeway and I was in the passenger seat, crying because I missed Rowyn so much.

All I wanted was comfort in that moment, and as I looked up, a hawk flew by right in front of our windshield. How was it even possible going seventy miles per hour?

I got a sense of comfort and peace every time I would see one. To me, it became a way she was showing me that she was with me.

She also started leaving me feathers at the most perfect times.

The first time I received one from her was about four weeks after she had passed.

Cody, Wyatt, Cassie, and many more of my family members had all found feathers and I hadn't yet. I was so sad and couldn't understand why Rowyn hadn't left me one.

My cousin Erin had been encouraging me to get out of the house, so we decided to go on a hike behind her home and get some fresh air.

I had just started driving short distances, so I dropped Wyatt off at school and headed over to her house a few miles away. It was a brisk fall morning and the fog was heavy. It had rained some the night before, so the gravel road was still wet.

We began our morning hike up in the hills of Skookumchuck. We stayed pretty quiet. My mood was so solemn, but it actually felt great to be outdoors breathing in the crisp morning air.

On our way up the large hill, I talked to Rowyn in my head.

*Sissy, please send me a sign, let me know you're with me right now, please. You have to make it obvious, honey, because I am pretty oblivious to everything right now.*

I truly needed a sign from her at that time. We hiked uphill until I had enough time to turn around, hike back and get Wyatt from school.

On our way back down the hill, I was watching my feet so my clumsy self wouldn't trip. There, right in my path, was a perfect, flawless feather.

The ground was damp and muddy, but this feather was dry, clean and perfect. It was like she had just put it in my path after I had asked her to. I knew strongly in my heart that this was a gift from above. I had asked her for a sign, and she heard me and placed the most beautiful feather right at my feet.

I began finding them in the most random of places. So random that I knew they were from Rowyn. They began to be so meaningful to me.

I loved hearing stories from my family and friends who would also find feathers they believed were from Rowyn.

Many of my family members wanted tattoos in honor of Rowyn. Cody and I decided to reserve a tattoo shop for a day to all get remembrance tattoos together. I walked into the parlor Lucky No 3 to book our appointments for my whole family to get Rowyn tattoos.

I was talking to the artist, telling him that most of my family would be getting feathers in her honor because she always left them for us. At that very moment, I looked at the floor and a perfect white feather was at my feet. IN THE TATTOO SHOP!

That was my sign from Rowyn that she liked the idea of us getting tattoos for her. I had put a lot of thought into what I wanted permanently on my body to represent and symbolize my daughter. . . the feather.

It came to me pretty easily. I decided to get the matching angel wing from her headstone down my arm with a few fallen feathers.

One of the fallen feathers was the exact one Rowyn had left me that day on my hike. Erin also felt so passionate about the feather we received that she got the same one tattooed on her arm.

I began receiving signs frequently, comforting me, reassuring me, and guiding me.

I just knew Rowyn was up in Heaven but still with me every day. She was cheering me on.

# Chapter Nineteen

### CASSIE

#### LOSING AGAIN

*"With pain comes strength."* -
*Author Unknown*

On November 2, 2014, my family picked up my two boys and me for a week visit in eastern Washington. It would be a week of time away from my reality here, but also a week of precious time with my grandma. As I mentioned before, she was dying of pancreatic cancer.

As difficult as it was for the whole family to make the phone call to hospice, one of their nurses was scheduled to arrive for our consult the very next day. I stayed at my brother and sister-in-law's home, but spent much of my days with my grandma. Visiting some of the times would be difficult considering I had two kids, one just eleven months old.

My Auntie Kay was her caretaker during the day, and my parents during the night. I now got to be part of that care. It gave me purpose, and given my job and recent history with death, I maybe had a little bit more of an ability to see what the outcome we were facing was.

Not only that, but possibly an ability to embrace it with a little more numbness.

Not that I was numb to what was happening, but I had just been through the worst experience in my life. I was no longer afraid of death, and I didn't want my grandma to be.

WHEN HOSPICE CAME, MY grandma was still in her lift recliner in the living room. We were able to get her up to walk with her walker, but she had to use the restroom in her bedroom. Her walker would not fit in her bathroom's tiny doorway.

In front of my grandma, we discussed what could be brought in the home to make her more comfortable.

At that point, she continued to talk about how she was going to get her strength back to make it to Virginia Mason to have surgery. Her tumor was covering a large blood vessel of her aorta. Had it been able to shrink enough during chemo, there was a chance it could be removed.

Unfortunately, we never got to that point.

I followed the consult nurse out to her car, and I asked her, "Is she starting the dying process?" I was blunt, afraid of the answer, but I wanted to know.

Everyone in the family felt this extreme guilt over contacting them, but I wanted to know the truth.

Both her family physician and the folks at the cancer center could not give this straight answer.

"Yes," she said. "She is starting it, and there is no timeline here because it is different for everyone."

That afternoon, I was with my grandma and my sister-in-law as we sat in her living room. I asked my grandma if she thought she was dying, and she said yes.

By the end of that week, I realized I didn't have anything I needed to rush back to western Washington for.

Easton was missing preschool, but that was not really that big of a deal. My plan for one week turned into an entire month. I even had to go clothes shopping while we were there because I had packed so little.

The hospital bed arrived the next day; my brother was there and we rearranged her bedroom to make room for it. It was so important to her to know exactly where everything was in her room still.

We made sure to keep those important things in plain view. She had a beautiful calendar beside her head with her gold brass cross and photographs all around the room of her family. She never lost her sense of humor through all of this.

It was just as we had been warned by hospice—once she gets in the hospital bed, she will likely not get out much more. We went from bedside bathroom breaks, to bedpans, to undergarments and eventually a catheter. She was failing so rapidly.

Her days consisted of sleeping for the most part, while one of us sat with her. We would be sure to put her favorite shows on, whether she was awake or not, play old music we knew she loved, and I read her scripture every day. Sometimes, she would just smile and squeeze my hand. It got harder and harder for her to talk.

During that time back at home, I realized the bad, dark days following the accident in September still followed me. I had a couple of days where functioning was just impossible.

My brother was irritated with me. "Why?" he said. "Who's going to take care of your kids when we're not here and you're like this?"

He didn't understand—I couldn't *not* be this way.

My therapist described to me back in the beginning that if I were to be hit by a bus, there would be many physically impairments you could see. The impairments I was struggling with were on the inside.

Painful to feel and even more painful to try and understand.

Even being away from home, I was in contact with Brynn quite often, each keeping tabs on how the other person was doing.

She had met with Kristi and began the first steps to starting the charity. She went through the bylaws, applied for our license, and asked me if I thought it would be a good idea to bring our friend Jen onboard.

I was in charge of drafting our sponsorship letter. I carried my niece's laptop back and forth to my grandma's for a couple weeks. Every time I would start on the letter and write a little bit, I would stop.

It was hard to dip back into that reality when I was face-to-face with this new one.

I was watching my grandmother slowly die in front of my eyes.

I watched my parents, brother and sister-in-law, aunt and cousin shed many tears.

I watched my niece and nephew struggle to understand the changes in my grandma and the decision that the kids just couldn't see her like that anymore.

Through it all, there was this toughness about me. I didn't *feel* tough, but I was being tough in the tough situation.

It was likely much easier for me considering I was on the most medication, though, but some of the time spent there with my grandma, I will never forget.

The nights I got to spend with my niece and nephew that fall are very meaningful to me. I even kicked some butt at the Xbox.

I cooked dinner at sometimes two households a day, which was productive for me. I was helping in a time that I felt useful and needed. It is a feeling I am not sure I would have made it through November without.

I will never forget the last day I spent at my grandma's with my parents, sister-in-law and my great-aunt and uncle.

We went through some old photographs. My great aunt talked about my grandma in such a beautiful way, and told stories I would have likely never heard.

I knew I was leaving the next day. Aaron had driven down for the weekend, and we were taking the boys home. This could possibly be ironic, but I choose to believe it is not.

While I was sitting with my grandma one day, I asked, "What is your favorite song?"

She responded by saying, "Merle Haggard, 'If We Make It Through December'." I put the song on my phone in iTunes, and we listened to it often.

Oddly enough, my grandmother passed away on December 1st, just minutes after I had gotten in the truck to leave. She surpassed all expectations, and made it to December.

# Chapter Twenty

## BRYNN

### LIVING WITH AN EMPTY HEART

*"Even the strongest of us have moments when the burdens of life seem to great. It's then that the Lord whispers to our hearts. . . Come to me all you who are weary and burdened, and I will give you rest."*
*Matthew 11:28*

My thoughts of Rowyn consumed everything I did. I didn't mind thinking about her; in fact, I never wanted her images to fade so I cherished every memory I had of her. . . except the accident flashbacks. The horrific images would creep into my thoughts and visions constantly. Everywhere I went, I had a video on repeat in my head of Rowyn's death. It was overwhelming me and I couldn't stop it. I would look out my window and all I could see was caution tape and Rowyn's teal and white polka dot jammies laying in the driveway. I would hear a siren while driving down the road and it would instantly take me back to standing in my yard hearing the sirens racing down my driveway. I would see any emergency vehicle and picture us sitting in the ambulance with our deceased daughter in my husband's arms. The visions were ruling me, but I didn't know how to shut them off. I would pray constantly asking God to remove the horrific images from my mind. I would have to stop what I was doing, close my eyes and just start praying, praying for the Lord to remove the terror from my memory. It would stop for a short period of time but I think when you witness something so catastrophic, it is forever engraved into your mind.

MONTHS HAD PASSED SINCE my daughter's death. I was still constantly searching.

In many ways, I was searching for anything or any way to connect to her.

I was reaching both hands in the air, grabbing for whatever strength God would give me to make it through each day.

I grew in my faith tremendously during that time. I prayed constantly, joined a weekly Bible study, and read the Bible daily. I felt empty inside, like I was missing a huge part of my heart, but God was bringing me comfort and strength that nobody else could give me.

A crisp October morning after dropping off Wyatt at preschool, I hopped into Cassie's car still in the school parking lot.

This had become our time where we would always have a few minutes in the mornings to chat.

Usually, our conversations were emotional, but we both were trying to be strong for one another.

We would cry together most mornings, hug, and pray, all while our little boys were just feet away in their classroom. God had placed this stronger connection between Cassie and me than ever before. I no longer just considered her a good acquaintance, but as family. We were now connected in this terrible, awful way, but I loved her so much.

As much as I was hurting for myself, I was also hurting for her. I knew her heart was hurting as much as mine, but in such a different way.

That morning was different.

Cassie was more upbeat than usual, and she seemed excited about something. She started the conversation with, "I've been thinking a lot about what we can do in honor of Rowyn. Something to raise money in her name to help other kids. Maybe a scholarship fund or something."

I loved the idea. We talked for a while about different ways we could raise money, but ideas kept coming easily to me during our conversation. It was as if they were from Rowyn or God just planting them in my train of thought.

We quickly came up with Raise for Rowyn, a non-profit that would provide assistance for other families suffering from the loss of a child.

We decided we did not want to be limited in the ways we could raise funds. I wanted to host charity events of all kinds, not just to raise funds but to raise awareness and spirits, as well.

Child death was much more common than I ever realized until it happened to me.

I wanted to help raise awareness that these accidents do happen all the time. I wanted to also help these other families that were suffering from tragedy.

Our morning conversation had given me excitement, and I had a little happiness for the first time in months. Our thirty-minute talk had given me something I could put positive focus on.

My only hesitation. . . could we handle this?

I knew nothing about starting a charity or a non-profit and neither did Cassie, but it felt so right. For the first time since Rowyn's passing, I felt joy about something.

We could make a difference in other families' lives. I didn't know how we were going to make this happen, but I was determined. I prayed about it throughout the day and that evening. I just was so lost and needed guidance.

I prayed all day. "Lord, if this is what I am supposed to be doing then lead me there. Please, lay out the path for Cassie and me if this is what you want us to be doing."

THAT EVENING, I SHARED the news with my husband. I was so excited to tell him about everything Cassie and I had discussed.

After sharing all of our plans and ideas, Cody seemed to love the idea of starting a non-profit in Rowyn's honor.

We both knew that's what our baby girl would have wanted from us.

The excitement from our conversation quickly turned to the awkward silence that so often filled our home.

"So, when are you planning on going back to work?" he asked.

I hesitated to answer. I didn't know what to tell him. He had went back to work a month after the accident, but I was still not ready. I was scared, nervous, and so anxious about it.

"I don't know, Cody. I've just been focusing on making it through a day let alone going back to work and facing the public."

My job was so different than his. He could work in solitude and not talk to people about losing our daughter. I felt completely exposed at my job. I wasn't ready for the questions and people staring at me.

"I have panic attacks going to the grocery store! Do you think I can handle going to work and having one-on-one conversations with people?" I snapped.

"Well, you need to do something, and you need to do it soon," he snapped back. "We have bills coming in left and right."

My eyes welled with tears. I knew he was right, but I wasn't ready.

I had to prep myself for hours before I went anywhere away from home. Clearly, he didn't understand at all how I was feeling. He didn't know what anxiety felt like or meant.

My mind started racing. I was thinking of my morning routine going back to work. I would be exhausted for the day after just getting ready, reapplying my makeup over and over because I couldn't stop crying. Having to go through every morning at 8:18 and recovering from that meltdown.

Working in an environment where I was used to sharing my life with my clients, I could not even fathom talking about this, or my life now. What would I even talk about without crying?

The honest truth was I used to always talk about my kids. All I was consumed with was pain now and I didn't want to share that with people.

The tears started flowing. I felt completely overwhelmed with just the idea of going back to work, and Cody did not understand at all.

THE CONVERSATION OF ME going back to work soon took over the evening topic around the dinner table.

This was ultimately affecting our marriage.

We had so much strain from just dealing with the accident and adding another topic to argue about didn't make it easier.

We were grieving completely differently.

He felt better by going to work and getting out of the house, where I wanted to just stay home and not get too far from Rowyn's room or things.

He could go about his day working with the guys and not talking about it, but I felt like that's all I was consumed by. If someone even made eye contact with me, I was going to break down.

I was clinging to my faith and growing my relationship with God, and he was clinging to a Busch Lite can after work.

I hated it, hated everything.

I couldn't believe this had become our reality. I felt like I had lost nearly everything I cared about, except my son. He was what kept me going on many mornings that I didn't want to get out of bed.

I couldn't let my depression affect how I was as a parent. I would not allow myself to sabotage his childhood because I was a disaster.

Pastor Jim had warned Cody and I on that dreaded day of Rowyn's passing. I remembered him saying, "This will be the most challenging thing your marriage will ever go through. Don't let the Devil win! He wants to wreck your marriage and everything he can."

I clung to the words, "Don't let the Devil win." I wasn't going to let that son of a bitch take anything else from me. He already had done enough damage and damn it, I wasn't going down without a fight.

So, I prayed. "Lord, give me strength to fight these battles against my depression, my marriage, fears, and anxieties."

# Chapter Twenty One

CASSIE

RAISE FOR ROWYN

*"You are a piece of the puzzle of someone else's life. You may never know where you fit, but others will fill the holes in their lives with pieces of you."*
*Bonnie Arbon*

As we made our way through December, I joined Brynn, Kristi and Jen in my first Raise for Rowyn meeting inside Starbucks on a weeknight.

That evening, we were focused on the run, dinner and auction we had planned for April 18, 2015.

The other girls had secured our venue in November while I was away, and Brynn had applied for our 501(c) 3.

I had finally completed the sponsor letter, and we had our friend Megan working on creating a website. Our goal was to go live with the website on January 10, 2015.

There we were, just four women, with an idea and a passion. Rowyn was heavy on our minds during all of this, but it was an exciting endeavor we were embarking on.

Somehow, it almost felt like it was coming together all too easily.

Getting through the holidays was also on the radar.

Christmas would be different, somber, and I imagined just how difficult that time would be for Brynn and Cody. Fortunately, we had our kids to force us into Christmas.

I would be dishonest if I said it was not a good Christmas, but it was certainly not an ordinary one for us.

Just after Christmas, Brynn and I had a meeting with the general manager of the Lucky Eagle Hotel and Casino in Rochester, Washington. Brynn used to work there for years, and their outpouring of support for her family during this tragic time had been so unbelievable. We were looking for a partnership, someone who could supply the food for our dinner event in April.

We were planning on 200 guests, at fifty-five dollars a ticket. We didn't need anything fancy, but to our surprise, John Setterstrom would do just about anything for Brynn and this cause.

We left his office grinning and giddy in the elevator that morning because we knew with them behind us, we could do this much easier.

"This is the happiest I have been since Rowyn passed away," Brynn told me in the car.

It was such a special time because it was exciting for us. In all the grief we were fighting every single day, wondering what to do with our lives, we were now on a mission to create a legacy for Rowyn.

Once the website went live and the sponsorship letters went out, we were on our way. Money and items started pouring into our mailbox, and we couldn't believe the amount of support we were receiving.

Even companies we didn't contact were sending us money. We hadn't even gotten our 501(c) 3 yet, but people didn't care. They wanted to help us.

Before long, we were able to place an order for Raise for Rowyn shirts, our first merchandise purchase. We were feeling good, a little intimidated at times, but for the most part we were feeling like things were being accomplished.

In between all of this excitement, there were still some bad days.

One I remember very vividly was a Tuesday.

As I mentioned before, Tuesdays are a harder day in the week for me. I had taken Logan to daycare and Easton to school. I stopped by the local post office to mail a couple of thank you cards to some sponsors.

It had been a difficult morning already, with a four-year-old and a one-year old; even getting out of the house in my grief-stricken state was a challenge.

As I looked across the seat at the cards, I reached for my purse.

*Where was it? Where was my stupid fucking purse?*

It was a day for the F-word, for sure. I had forgotten it. I had left my house without everything; just my kids and those cards made it inside the car.

I was about to blow my tear gaskets because the simple irritation that would come for anyone in that situation is just too overwhelming for someone who is in mine.

Just then, I looked up and saw Sheri, Brynn's mother-in-law. She carried a box and was heading into the post office. When we made eye contact, I rolled down my window because she headed toward me.

In an instant, those gaskets blew. I tried to fight the tears with eye-squinting and silence, but that never works.

She asked me if I was okay, and I just said yeah, I had just forgotten my stupid purse.

She offered to mail what I had went there to send, but I declined.

I don't think she believed me, because she asked again. "Are you sure you're okay?"

I nodded, but the flood gates that opened were far from being stopped.

As she walked away into the post office, I felt far too weak to be driving.

However, I had to get out of that parking lot.

I was mortified.

As I pulled out to the backroad, that feeling came over me, just as it did in my office back in October.

My hands began to go numb, and I felt lightheaded and short of breath. I pulled onto a side road and parked. I needed to get myself together so I could go back home. It was a bad day.

I have had a lot of these in the last year, some harder than others. Some, I'm able to make it to work, but eventually have to leave. Some, I've made it to the town I work in, and then have to turn around. The only thing that soothes me is sleep, and when I lie down after these episodes, let me tell you I can sleep.

Somewhere in the midst of our planning, Brynn was reached out to by a local burger joint called The Burger Claim.

The people there wanted to do a fundraiser for us. They wanted to donate the day's revenue to our charity. We thought this would be a great thing.

Something local to us, somewhere we could start to face the public.

We made some flyers for the tables, and I created a newsletter to be passed out to customers.

After speaking with the manager, Rene, I knew I had to be there that day to greet customers.

Brynn was not quite prepared yet. We had been in the public eye for months, or at least it felt like that, but conversing with people seemed scary for us both. A newfound anxiety had imbedded in both our lives since the accident.

She went to work that day, and Easton, and I went to The Burger Claim.

To my surprise, the doors would not stop opening. The lines were out the door, in fact, and the tables were full of people. It was unreal. I never expected to see anything near that.

As I quickly began sending pictures to the Raise for Rowyn team, Brynn realized she needed to be there, too. It was just too exciting for our charity, and many of the supporters were hers. She rushed over with her Raise for Rowyn shirt on, and we greeted and visited with customers until about 10:00 P.M.

The drive-thru was backed up six cars deep at times, and people were handing us money left and right. We made over $1,000 just in cash that had been given to us personally.

We were left dumbfounded.

By means of Facebook and a few flyers, we realized how many people were behind us and our cause.

What would Raise for Rowyn be able to do next?

# Chapter Twenty Two

BRYNN

IT'S ALL IN THE WRITING

*After your season of suffering, God in all his grace will restore, confirm, strengthen and establish you. 1 Peter 5:10*

After a few months of being off work, I slowly started getting back into a routine.

I started with shorter work days and sometimes only worked one or two days per week. It was something, though, and Cody seemed to be appeased, so our home life was slowly getting back to normal, too.

The holidays were close approaching, and I was absolutely dreading them. Christmas used to be my favorite time of year, but I found myself ignoring everything I loved about it before.

The decorating, the cooking, buying gifts, family, and especially making it special for my kids. . . I felt like I couldn't be excited about any of it.

I had no daughter to go Christmas shopping for anymore. I couldn't hardly step foot into a store without having a panic attack being surrounded by all these gifts that I would have loved to buy for Rowyn.

I wanted to do something special for her.

I decided the only tree I was going to get into decorating was one for Rowyn's grave. Cousin Nikki found the perfect hot pink girly tree with little white lights already attached. I decorated it with teal Christmas ornaments, her favorite color. It was absolutely precious, and it was all I felt I could do for her.

Our family had planned on a time Christmas morning to meet at the cemetery. I did not have the energy in me to plan anything, so cousins, Nikki and Robin, once again planned a special tribute for Rowyn. We did our usual morning breakfast at our Aunt Lynda's house.

The kids played, opened gifts, we took some photos, but the room did not have its usual joyous feeling. I wasn't up for staying long; I was trying so hard to keep it together. I truly didn't want to burst into tears in front of all the kids on such a special day for them. I felt like I could lose it at any moment.

After breakfast, we snuck out fairly quickly. I barely made it to the car and started sobbing.

"It's just not the same. . .  it will never be the same again. I feel no joy without Rowyn being a part of Christmas morning with us," I cried.

I sobbed the whole way to the cemetery.

As we pulled in, some of our family was already there waiting for us. I took my tissue and tried to clean up the mascara that had streaked my face. *Sunglasses it's going to be on this cloudy day, because there is no fixing this disaster.*

Nikki and Robin had brought balloons for everybody. Nobody really talked, we just all stood around Rowyn's grave and stared at it.

I have never heard silence like that before from my family. I, of course, was crying, but trying to be discreet about it. Cars were pulling in one after another, just like the day of her funeral.

Our large, loving family was all there to honor our baby Rowyn and support Cody and me.

I was so grateful for all of the support. How special that even all the little cousins and kids were there on their holiday, still wanting to remember and cherish Rowyn.

Uncle Rob said a prayer aloud. The tears and sobs were surrounding me with so much love and so much sadness all at the same time. We each released a balloon for her that morning.

It was such a painful morning but a beautiful way for our family to show love for our missing baby girl.

The emptiness still consumed me daily. All I could think about was Rowyn. I missed so much taking care of a baby and having a little best friend.

Wyatt was growing up so fast and really didn't want to hang out with his momma anymore. He always wanted to be with his daddy or the guys.

I became jealous that he would rather spend time with Cody than me. I was so lonely and wanted another child desperately. I knew no child would ever replace my bond and love for Rowyn, but I yearned for that love and connection again.

I prayed daily to get pregnant. It just seemed like it was taking forever.

Once I got pregnant, I knew it would seem like forever until the baby was there. I practically begged God every night to bless us with another baby girl. I would talk to Rowyn, too, and make sure she knew Mommy would never replace her. She was my best friend, my everything, but I wanted her to help God pick out the perfect little sister for us. I knew this would come in God's timing, but I was impatiently waiting.

THAT FEBRUARY, I PLANNED a trip for just Cody, Wyatt, and I to go to Hawaii. We needed to reconnect as a family after everything we had been through.

Cody was not very excited about the idea of spending money on a vacation, but it was important to me. I found a great deal online to Aulani Disney resort in Hawaii.

I was so excited to take Wyatt and spend quality time with the two most important people in my life. On our way to the airport, we made a stop at Rowyn's grave to bring her some fresh flowers.

This was always emotional for Cody and me, but I could not leave without going to talk to her there. I had designed a beautiful vase of flowers for her. It had become something I spent time thinking about and preparing, beautiful bouquets for her that had meaning to them.

I picked Tiger lilies because they reminded me of a tropical vacation, and a mix of Gerbera daisies, her signature flower. As we pulled away, I couldn't help but feel like I was leaving her behind. . . I was missing something.

Our trip was unusually easy-going. We were expedited through lines at the airport, never had to wait or hustle. It was as smooth-sailing as it could possibly be. The pilot even invited Wyatt back into the cockpit with him. He loved the experience.

We sat in the middle row of the plane with four seats together. The one next to me was empty, but in my mind, baby Rowyn was sitting there.

After arriving in Hawaii and checking into our room, we decided we weren't completely satisfied with our location or view. We were on the 16th floor with a grand view of the parking lot and really far away from the beach.

I normally would not say anything about it, but something kept urging me to call and check if another room was available. After a few minutes of the persistent urge consuming me, I called the front desk. I politely asked if there were any lower-floor rooms available or possibly anything closer to the beach and pool. The receptionist politely told me most likely not since all those rooms were requested in advance, but that she would check.

After being placed on hold shortly, the receptionist came back on. "We actually do have a ground-level room available, room 111."

The room couldn't have been more perfect! We were close to the beach, pools, restaurants, yet tucked away in a private jungle setting.

We could walk out the sliding glass door and not have to worry about taking an elevator anywhere. I had read that the number sequence 111 represents angels and is a heavenly number.

I couldn't help but believe my daughter had a hand in picking our room for us.

Every day, every night, everywhere we went, I was constantly looking for signs from Rowyn.

About halfway through our trip, I started to get very sad that I had not received any obvious, 'slap me in the face' signs from Rowyn. That night, I said a prayer asking for a sign from above. I needed to know Rowyn was with us. I then talked to Rowyn aloud. "Ro, please send Mommy a really obvious sign that you're here with us. Mommy is really oblivious, so I am asking you to make it a really obvious sign."

That night, Rowyn visited me in a dream. It was so real. I was driving and saw her in my rearview mirror, just the way it used to be. She was sitting in the middle of the backseat instead of the side, buckled into her car seat next to Wyatt.

When Rowyn was alive she never sat in the middle. I had moved Wyatt onto her side after she passed. I felt like she was saying to me in the dream, 'this is where I sit now'. I did not want to take my eyes off her. I was afraid if I glanced away she would be gone. I was driving and had to look away for a split second. When I looked back I couldn't believe it, but she was still there.

My dream jumped ahead and I was at our cousin's house. I walked into a birthday party, just Wyatt and I. There were a ton of people there, and I felt overwhelmed. I looked down and there she was again! She was standing right beside me, and I could not focus on anything else but her. Everyone else in the room blurred out at that time except my crystal-clear image of my baby. I picked her up and sat her on the counter in front of me. I was overjoyed to see her. I was in such shock she was there and started taking pictures of her with my phone, but when I would look at my phone, she wasn't there. I looked up and she was gone.

After waking up, I strongly knew this was a visitation from Rowyn. It was so vivid and clear; I could remember every little detail of the dream. I felt like she was reassuring me that she was with me everywhere I went. It was so real that I missed her so much more. It was like a little taste of what I used to have. I was so happy, but I cried off and on throughout the entire day just missing her. I would give anything to have her back.

CASSIE

THE LORD IS MY SHEPHERD

*"I was blind, but now I see" John 9:25*

With the charity pushing forward, so was Brynn's and my faith.

We were in church almost every single Sunday, reading the Bible, sharing verses. Brynn was attending a Bible study weekly and I had continued with my devotionals.

I loved finding God.

The day I saw God, I will never forget. I'm not sure if I mentioned it before, but it was my 'finding God 101 day'.

I felt like I was literally seeing the world for the first time through a new lens. God had gotten me through this, I know that much.

Once you get a taste of Him, you thirst for more.

To this day, I bring my Bible to work with me daily, I have a devotional calendar on my desk, and now I keep a four-minute Bible study book there, as well.

I listen to Christian music for the most part in my car. I crave uplifting words and inspiring stories, and encouragement from others who have been in difficult times.

I have been changed through this tragedy, and it has been the hardest thing that I have ever been through, and hope to ever have to go through.

But now, I know I could make it through anything because of my faith.

I'm a stronger woman.

I am not afraid to talk about my faith to other people, but I do not want to shove it down your throat, either.

When the accident first happened, and I was seen in the doctor's office, the doctor asked me, "Do you have a faith system in place?"

I responded with, "Well, I'm a Christian."

Despite what I said, I knew I wasn't a practicing Christian.

I had never read the Bible, only intended on it one day.

I never thought I would be able to even understand the language in it. It was so insignificant to my life at that time.

How stupid I feel for even making that statement.

How could I have made something so huge, the creation of my existence, insignificant?

Looking back at my life prior to the accident, there is so much I miss about myself and my personality. I know I'm different, I can feel it.

I loved to joke around, and I was social and bubbly even on a shitty day. I have been told by my mom that I am missing a sparkle from my eye now. I avoid people sometimes, groups can give me anxiety if I am not prepared, and Aaron says I am much more serious.

I hate that, feeling like I have lost so many parts to myself. I'm sure it's a common feeling among many people who have been through something big in their life.

For the longest time, I yearned to be the old Cassie, but I understand now that I am a forever-changed and new Cassie.

One thing the new Cassie has, though, is faith. It has allowed me to lead a better life as a human being and appreciate everything so much more.

When I started going to our church, it was as if the people there were old friends. They comforted and prayed for us before even knowing us. These people would literally do anything for us.

Still to this day, Aaron and I both feel like the members help us want to be better people. We feel good when we leave there, feel blessed.

I will still say that I wish I could go back to September 16, 2014, and change our plans and never end up in Brynn and Cody's driveway that morning.

I will say that until the day I die.

However, my friend pointed out to me that I am now living a better life because of what happened. It would be unfortunate for me to not share that thought with you.

I began to really start thinking as the charity grew before our eyes. *What is it that I really want to do with my life?*

I felt like I was starting to see options I had never considered before. I never wanted anything different before. I just wanted to get healthy so I could someday go back to supervision at work.

I remember being in therapy and Chris said to me, "You can do whatever you want to do. Maybe that job is not where your heart is anymore. Maybe it's not something you can even handle anymore. You can be whoever you want to be. What are some personality traits you want in yourself?"

It was like I was getting a clean slate. Things I had never considered before.

Just then, I thought back to a time just a couple of months before the accident.

My girlfriends and I were over at a friend's house when the question was asked, "What is the one thing you have always wanted to do in your life, but you haven't?"

Everyone's answers were very exciting to hear.

I answered by saying, "I have always wanted to write a book." I looked at Chris and said, "Well, I have always wanted to write a book, but I have never had anything to really say."

"I could see this being a book," she said. "I could see you and Brynn writing it together. You have a unique story, and you should tell it."

One night, we had met at the Scatter Creek Winery in Tenino for a Raise for Rowyn meeting. In my opinion, it was the best one yet because of the wine and the laid-back atmosphere.

Our team sat on a sectional couch with Megan, our web designer, and eventually called our graphic design artist, Adam, to come down for his help.

While Adam sat on the floor beside us strumming his guitar, we sipped wine and made even more progress with Raise for Rowyn. I told Brynn that night that I wanted to write a book about all of this, and she said she wanted to, as well.

Little did the two of us know, but God and Rowyn, would be laying this incredible opportunity at our feet soon enough.

# Chapter Twenty Four

BRYNN

AN EVENT TO REMEMBER

*"For I know the plans I have for you, declares the Lord, plans
to prosper you and not to harm you, plans to give you hope
and a future."*
*Jeremiah 29:11*

Our first big Raise for Rowyn charity events were soon approaching. I had a strong team of board members in place helping all along the way, preparing and planning, but I had never been so overwhelmed in all my life.

I mean overwhelmed in a good way, because I truly loved what I was doing, I felt like I was acting out my soul purpose almost. I was excited yet filled with so much anxiety leading up to the day.

Our events would be held on the day before Rowyn's second birthday.

We specifically chose this date to honor her. I wanted something that we could do every year the Saturday closest to her birthday, to not only remember her but to always remind the community why this charity started in the first place.

It had only been less than seven months since she had passed, yet there I was planning two major events during an extremely emotional time for myself and family.

On one hand, it felt so amazing to be planning these major charity events and to have already helped other families, but my brain was boggled with so much to do. I knew it had to be God's work guiding me, because I still had many days where even attempting to load the dishwasher or take a shower seemed overwhelming.

My phone became a constant source of stress for me. It would be chiming all day with texts, emails, and phone calls that would overwhelm me.

I started putting it on silent for a few hours at a time so I could focus on getting anything accomplished.

Never in my old life did I imagine this was where I would be or what I would be doing.

Cassie and I began spending long days together, working on the charity and planning our events. It became a source of healing for me as well as added stress.

*Did I take on too much? I don't know if I will be able to keep composed during these events. What was I thinking?*

Sometimes, we would spend more hours in a day working on Raise for Rowyn than we would at our real jobs. We shared our future plans and goals for the charity, and it seemed like our visions always went hand-in-hand.

As unstable and crazy as we felt, we made a great team. We agreed that growing our charity was where we wanted to be. Another goal we shared was writing a book together.

SOON AFTER OUR CONVERSATION regarding the book, I was working at the salon. Little did I know I was chatting to a successful local writer.

Our conversation started out with small talk but quickly evolved into book talk. I wasn't working many hours at that point in time, nor had I ever seen her in the salon before, so I felt like God crossed our paths that day for a specific reason.

I went home that night and prayed about it. I knew God was telling me something, and I wanted to make sure I wasn't overthinking the book dream and then the encounter with her.

It didn't take long before God's answer came clear to me, and that became the beginning for Cassie and me to start writing our book.

This was a journey we never planned on taking, but God just kept placing these perfect opportunities and people in our paths.

We were going to share our story, both sides, while gracefully healing and hopefully helping many individuals that may suffer from either situation. I constantly prayed for guidance and this is where He led me, giving me step-by-step directions along the way.

During the morning of April 17, 2014, we hosted a 5K run and mini street fair, and that evening we held a semi-formal dinner and auction at a beautiful small-town local venue.

Tickets were sold out in advance, and we served 200 people that evening for dinner.

With a combination of both events, in one day we had raised over $60,000. This was a huge success for Raise for Rowyn.

We never expected to be able to raise that much funding in one day. The events went off perfectly, and I couldn't have been more satisfied with how things kept magically coming together. I knew it was God and Rowyn orchestrating the whole thing. It flowed too seamlessly for it not to be.

My spirits were lifted, and I was feeling so proud of the legacy we had created all in honor of my baby girl. Nervously, each one of my team members stood and gave a speech that evening.

They were heartfelt and sincere, showing love and compassion, not just for Rowyn but the charity and everything it was linked to. I was last. I had been keeping a secret, and it was time to share it.

The calmness of the Lord filled me and my anxieties went away. I was filled with a sense of peace and calmness as I took the stage. I wasn't sure how I was going to share my news, but I knew God and Rowyn would guide me and it would just flow the way it was supposed to.

During my speech, near the end, I revealed that I was three months pregnant. I was riding on a high that evening, could feel the love in the room. Rowyn and God's presence were felt by everyone. I even had complete strangers tell me they could feel God with us that evening. It was truly magical.

Unfortunately, the night's high ended abruptly. The following day was Rowyn's birthday, the day I had been dreading for a long time. I had expected to be emotional, but I wasn't prepared for the high I was on the evening before to end so quickly and be replaced by an overwhelming feeling of pain, grief, and hopelessness. This was the grief roller coaster everyone warned me about.

I felt completely unstable all over again. I went out to Rowyn's garden at my home.

I had no energy but it was such a beautiful day out, so I decided to spend some time working in her remembrance garden. I took out some fresh flowers to plant, a mini shovel and gardening gloves.

Walking out there by myself, I knew I was going to get emotional, and I was honestly ready to just have a good cry. I had been holding it in for weeks, trying to keep it together for my Raise for Rowyn events.

I sat on the garden bench and just stared at the flowers. A white butterfly came by and kept landing near me.

*Here it comes. . .*

I lost it. I cried for a good twenty minutes, just sitting there by myself. This was not like a little weep, I was sobbing uncontrollably. I was so heartbroken and lonely for my daughter.

I would give anything to hold that little angel again. I didn't get much accomplished in her garden. I managed to trim back some ferns and set the sprinklers, but that's about all I could manage to do.

To be honest, I needed that alone time to just break down.

As I sat there basking in my sadness, I couldn't help but think that I should be preparing for her birthday party right then. I had already envisioned the party theme before she passed. I loved decorating, and I planned on doing an over-the-top strawberries and cream theme. Pink and girly, strawberries on top of each cupcake and strawberry milkshakes.

With my imagination taking over, picturing all the details I had planned, I just continued to break down. I wanted to know what they do in Heaven. How do they celebrate birthdays up there? I just wanted to know what she was doing. Couldn't God just give me a little glimpse of how they were celebrating for her up there?

Later that day, I planned on going out to the cemetery to take Rowyn some fresh flowers and balloons.

When I arrived, I saw that many people had already been there and left flowers, cards, and little gifts. It warmed my heart to know my daughter was loved by so many. She was still fresh in people's minds, even seven months after her passing. I am proud of how powerful my daughter is and am happy I got the privilege of being Rowyn's mommy. I look up to her in many ways and am always inspired to be a better person because of her. I see her love still continuing to spread and how she affects people's lives in a positive way.

For being two years old, she sure had already accomplished a lot. With that, I am so honored that I got to spend her seventeen months of life with her, even though it ended in a lot of pain. I wouldn't trade that time for anything. I was sure every birthday was going to be difficult for me, but I knew she would continue to bless people for many years to come.

As our charity was growing, so was my pain. I found that releasing my innermost feelings through writing helped to ease some of the heartache. Cassie and I started blogging our feelings and sharing our experiences. It was hard to bare it all, the good, bad, and ugly, but we quickly realized how many other grieving families it was helping.

Our blogging was connecting us with families all over the country, as well as helping us release our pain.

Writing was helping in more ways than I ever expected it to.

# Chapter Twenty Five

## CASSIE

### RUN FOR ROWYN

*"Run with purpose"*
*1 Corinthians 9:26*

March was coming to an end, and we found ourselves extremely busy getting everything ready for our big event.

This was really becoming a full-time job for four people, who all had other real jobs and young children.

Rowyn's room had become Raise for Rowyn headquarters, and it was filled with silent auction baskets, raffle items, decorations, and the shirts. We ordered brown bags and a custom Raise for Rowyn stamp to mark them. Teal and cream tissue paper for stuffing. We wanted everything to be Rowyn's style. For as small as she was, Rowyn definitely had style.

We had a few things to stuff in each bag, along with the shirts.

One evening, Brynn, Jen and I were in Rowyn's bedroom stuffing race bags. Something we would spend more than one evening doing.

Kristi had created labels for each bag so we were able to stuff them with the right size and color shirt. She definitely kept us organized in this event.

A friend of all of ours, Stefanie, came over to help stuff bags, as well. We thought it was so nice of her to be there helping us, and she had also known Rowyn pretty well.

"We should just make you a board member, Stef," Brynn said.

We all agreed it was a good idea. We needed the extra hands and heart on our team.

We knew we couldn't just add anyone; it had to be someone who would share the passion with us.

Stefanie accepted, and Raise for Rowyn grew from four to five.

A few weeks later, we were at Brynn's house for a quick little photo shoot. We decided the website needed to see all the faces behind Raise for Rowyn, not just Brynn's and mine.

If anyone thought we were getting this done alone, boy were they wrong.

A coworker of Brynn's, but a friend of all of ours, was to be our photographer for the day.

She came and took some photos of us.

"Sheri would be a good board member, right?" I said to Brynn.

"Yeah, I think she would be a great one."

It was not long after that when we had to load two trailers full of the collected items over the past few months. Sheri offered to come and help us because the rest of our team had to be at work.

That day, Brynn asked her if she would like to join our Raise for Rowyn team. She accepted, and just two days before our biggest event of the year, we were lucky to go from five to six.

The Friday before our big event, we started decorating and setting up tables in the venue, Campbell and Campbell's. It is a gorgeous place, with sandstone walls and good lighting.

Brynn has some good memories of Rowyn there just a couple of weeks before she passed away.

The team that came to help that day was unbelievable. I wouldn't be able to mention them all if I tried, as it literally took a team.

Many of the people were our family members. There were so many items in the silent auction to display we actually ran out of room. Items ranged from gift certificates to large pieces of furniture.

As if we didn't already feel blessed enough, more items kept being dropped off last-minute.

Looking around the room at all the things people had given to Raise for Rowyn to support this cause was breathtaking.

A chill ran through my body when the sunset hit a photograph of Rowyn with wings on each side of her. We felt her with us all day, and there she was glowing in the room. We had arrived at Campbell's that morning to set up at nine, and when we left, it was already 10 P.M.

I headed home to greet the rest of my family who had come into town that day. I was on a high for how great the place looked.

Going to sleep that night required a few Coors Lights first.

The crazy part was we had a whole other event happening in the morning, and we needed to be there at six to set up. Our families, close friends and several church members took part in this event with us.

When I woke up that morning, I felt a little anxious. I said my prayers and prepared myself for an incredibly busy and likely emotional day ahead.

When the people started arriving, it was really overwhelming. There were just so many. Lucky Eagle Casino had their food truck parked and were whipping up breakfast sandwiches for donation only.

We had friends manning our raffle tables, selling raffle tickets, and church family Tony and Teah DJ'ing.

At the starting line, our board members all held balloons with our children while Teah led us in prayer.

When she was finished, we released our balloons to Heaven. I had tears rolling down my face, puddles under my sunglasses. With my youngest Logan in my arms, and Easton at my side, Brynn and I hugged.

It was an emotional moment for me. *This woman still really does forgive me. She is so brave, and I love her so much.*

The racers were off, and in the meantime, the street was filling up with a petting zoo, a balloon man, a coloring station, a bounce house, face painting, temporary tattoos, a fire truck, a S.W.A.T. truck and a popcorn stand.

There were a couple of minor mishaps with our course, but as a whole, the event was extremely successful for Raise for Rowyn.

How the hell did we manage to pull it off?

I have no idea, but that's God for you.

# Chapter Twenty Six

BRYNN

MY LIFE UNEXPECTED

*"People can plan what they want to do but it is the Lord who guides their steps."*
Proverbs 16.9

A mother from Texas reached out to me after hearing our story. She shared with me her situation, which was very similar to mine. She had lost her son at home in the same terrible way—a tragic accident, but with her husband behind the wheel. She lost her son a short few months before I lost Rowyn.

It wasn't long before we began messaging, sharing our struggles with each other. It was therapeutic to connect so strongly with another mom battling the same battle.

We mailed Christmas gifts for each other's family and have remained in contact ever since. She became the mother to me that I could message and vent to when I needed and I knew she would understand, always offering kind words and giving me hope. That's the grieving mother I wanted to be for others.

Word about our charity spread quickly. I began receiving emails and personal messages on Facebook from other mothers who had lost their children. I began connecting with these moms on a regular basis. Sometimes daily, I would receive a message from another mother sharing her grief with me.

It was heartbreakingly painful to hear their stories on how they lost their child and how they were dealing with the grief, but at the same time it was so nice to connect to anyone who knew firsthand the hell I was going through. I took on these mommies pain just as my own.

My heart would ache after reading another message about a child passing. It was terrible, heart-wrenchingly ugly. I don't understand why so many little children go before they should, and we're just left here to go on without them.

As painful as it was for me, it was also giving me a purpose. I was helping these other women, inspiring them and giving them hope to keep going, keep going for our children in Heaven. They would always be watching us from above, and we needed to make our angel babies proud. God gave me the strength to be strong when I needed to be. I felt like I was leading these mommies to God, or at least to grace. There was a bond between us that most people wouldn't understand, nor would we want anyone to. A connection on a deeper level, sharing our pain and grief with one another.

The charity continued to grow, and so did I. I was approaching the time in pregnancy where I could find out the sex of our baby.

Of course, I wanted to know. Cody and I both desperately wanted another little girl.

This had become a daily prayer in our home, practically begging God for another little girl. I openly admitted that I was going to be so ticked at God if He didn't answer my prayer. I would never turn away from my faith, but I let God know that I was going to be really upset if I didn't get my way.

I felt guilty saying it, but it was the truth. I had become comparable to my unreasonable four-year-old regarding the matter, but I felt like He owed me a girl after everything we had been through.

I had scheduled my ultrasound appointment, and I mentally started to prepare myself that it may be a boy. Cody's demanding work schedule conflicted with the appointment.

At that point, after all the anticipation, I did not want to cancel and have to reschedule.

My curiosity was killing me.

Since Cody couldn't make the appointment, we decided to do a gender reveal that evening with our immediate family and all find out together. I knew this would be an emotional time regardless of what the sex was, but I wanted to share that moment with our family.

My cousin and sister-in-law went with me to the appointment. I paid the extra money out of pocket to have a more detailed ultrasound. We told the tech right away that we wanted the sex to remain a surprise so we could all find out together later on, but if he 'accidentally' happened to show the private region on the screen that would be fine.

The ultrasound was amazing. The baby looked healthy and was developing the way it should be, but he never 'accidentally' slipped up and revealed the gender. He really wanted to keep us guessing, so as he entered the data in the computer, he was entering extra letters to throw us off. He printed out the ultrasound pic and sealed it in an envelope.

Our anticipation really grew. We had the results in our possession, and we could so easily just open it and find out. We could pretend that we were surprised later on and nobody would have to know. The temptation was there, but we never peeked. We truly wanted it to be special, and I most of all wanted to share the moment with Cody.

That evening, my immediate family and a few of my closest friends came to our home to reveal the surprise together.

We had given the ultrasound results to a cake decorator, and she was the only person who knew what it was. She made us a cake. Was it going to be pink or blue on the inside?

We all gathered around, filled with excitement and anticipation.

As I cut into the cake with Cody by my side, it revealed light pink filling pouring out. We were having a little girl.

In that moment, I was flooded with emotions. I felt overjoyed to know God answered my prayers and was sending me the gift of another little girl. I also felt an instant fear, wondering what I would do if something were to happen to her. I felt sadness that Rowyn was not there to celebrate becoming a big sister, and I felt guilt that Rowyn may feel replaced.

The rush of emotions overwhelmed me, and I started to well up with tears. Looking around the room, there was not a dry eye there. I think we all were feeling the same way. I was filled with fear from so many different things, but I wasn't going to let it stop me from celebrating our new little girl coming into the world.

I am constantly reflecting back on the last year since losing Rowyn. My life now is never what I expected it to be. I thought I had it all planned out and honestly, I thought my path was set before experiencing this tragedy.

I had married the man who always had my heart, bought a beautiful home together to start a family, had the career I was passionate about with a steady clientele, and had healthy children.

I felt like that was how I would spend the rest of my days, raising my kids in our small town of Tenino and continuing to be a stylist until retirement.

Now, I have realized that my destiny is truly out of my control. I don't know where my path is going; I have left that up to God. It all works out the way He planned it anyway.

I don't know what tomorrow will bring, let alone what five years from now will be.

My goals and values have completely changed. By nature, I have always been driven and desired the quality things in life, but before, that consisted of the fancy rigs to drive around, the nice leather handbag, ridiculously expensive cowboy boots, and the 'bigger is better' mentality.

I still like myself a nice pair of cowboy boots and I am sure I always will, but now I just don't value those things as much as I did before.

I value quality time with my family.

I value keeping a clean and happy home for my children and husband.

I value going to church on Sundays with Cassie and our families.

I value going to my son's soccer games and field trips.

I have, in many ways, been extremely humbled from my experience.

God has taken me down a path I didn't expect to be on. I now am running a rapidly growing non-profit charity, expecting my third child at 32 years old, and I no longer want to work out of the home because I don't want to miss a second with my children.

I have no idea where my career path is going.

I still love my job, but my passion has changed. It is now helping these other families that are experiencing the same challenges as me. That is essentially where my heart is.

I would give anything to have my daughter back, and that will never change. But after where my life has gone in the last year, I must say I am happy with the person I have become and where God has led me.

I have struggled but given it my all to get through the most challenging situation anyone could be faced with, and I am surviving.

My faith has continued to grow, and I like where God has taken me.

I have completely evolved into this better version of myself, a version I didn't know ever existed. I didn't know how to be empathetic before, almost to a fault.

People would tell me their sad stories, but I just didn't have that sensitivity in me.

Now I am sympathetic and empathetic to every sad situation I hear about.

My relationship with my husband has grown, as well. We have gone through absolute Hell together, and most couples don't recover from the loss of a child.

It has been so challenging, but I feel now more than ever that we will always make it through anything. He has seen me at my lowest of lows, riding on the crazy bus, and I have seen his darkest sides, as well. However, we still have managed to come out together.

I used to pray that my husband would grow closer to the Lord, not knowing how that would ever happen. Now I see this whole new man he has become.

We can openly talk about our faith, he joins me in church, and he now makes living for God a priority in his life. He has been so humbled yet he's evolved into this man I never expected him to be, and I love him more now than ever before.

Our bond has changed.

He is Rowyn's only other parent, and only he can understand how it feels to have lost her.

Sure, his grief as a father and mine as a mother are different, as well as our roles in the accident, but we both come back together as Rowyn's parents.

This past year has been the most challenging time of my life and marriage but after making it this far, I feel stronger than ever in my commitment to my husband and the Lord.

The planner in me wants to map out my next chapter in life, but for now, I am really just leaving it in God's hands.

I pray for Him to guide me every day down the path He has for me.

So far, every opportunity for the charity to grow has just been placed before me. I know that's where He wants me to be right now. I am just His worker here on Earth. He has this journey for me, and I am just doing His will.

Rowyn is right by my side leading me, as well. Her powerful soul has changed people's lives all over the world, and she is continuing to do so. I know this is what I need to be doing as well, always and forever honoring my daughter's life while assisting other families experiencing the same tragedy. I know she would be proud. She was special and I felt it all along, and now I have devoted to spend the rest of my days raising awareness and never letting people forget her. She was and will always be my angel baby.

# Chapter Twenty Seven

## CASSIE

### AN INTIMATE NIGHT

*"The Lord is my light and my Salvation."*
*Psalm 27:1*

There was literally no time to go all the way home to freshen up before the event, so Brynn, Stefanie and I stayed behind at Campbell and Campbell's.

Brynn needed a moment to herself, so Stefanie, our friend Elder and I walked next door to the Scatter Creek Winery.

I kicked off my shoes, sat on the couch and sipped a glass of wine.

It was then that we heard the news. There was a tragic accident similar to ours that morning in Marysville, WA. It was devastating to think about what they were going through in those moments.

It was also a realization of how far we had come. We decided not to tell Brynn.

While we sat there, I practiced my speech in front of the girls. Not long after that, Brynn called to say she was lonely and to come back.

Stefanie and I walked back to Campbell's, where we began getting ready with Brynn, her cousin, and a good friend. It seemed like no time at all when the rest of our team appeared, our DJ Mark, and our MC of the night, our amazing pastor, Jim.

He arrived, and we all did a champagne toast together following the prayer he led us in.

The room started to fill up, and it was amazing. Everyone looked so dolled up, and was happy to be there with us. There were tears and hugs from lots of people.

I had friends I've known for over twenty-five years there, and even their parents were in attendance. The support for both Brynn and I, at this intimate, personal venue, was so meaningful. I do not think I will ever fully have words to express that.

The dinner was wonderful, the silent auction bids were growing, and beer and wine were selling.

Pretty soon, it was time for our speeches. Kristi started it off with how hers became such a huge role in Raise for Rowyn from day one.

Then Jen spoke about her passion for the charity, thanking some key people and how it felt to see how far Brynn and I had come.

It was my turn. I had focused my speech on the topic of teamwork. I did that because it was the real word behind what Raise for Rowyn had evolved into, with an idea that was brought forward in October. But first and foremost, I of course had to say something about Rowyn. It was the hardest thing to spit out in front of two hundred people, including her closest family members.

"There are few days in a person's life that they will never forget," I said. "For me, it was my wedding day, the birth of my two children, and of course, Rowyn. I will never be able to put into words what Raise for Rowyn means to me emotionally." That was where I stopped, my eyes squinted, my body clenched and I tried as hard as I could to stop the tears. To my surprise, I did it. I went on to say, "But in order to keep things upbeat tonight, I want to talk about something else."

Getting that speech off my chest was freeing. Just as every blog feels, and every time we help a family. Brynn went next, and I don't think anyone left that night without realizing just how beautiful, inside and out, that woman really is. Her speech left even me in awe. She shared with the audience the news of her pregnancy by saying, "Raise for Rowyn is not the only thing growing. My belly is, too." She winged the entire speech and gracefully spoke of how the charity has helped keep Rowyn so alive.

We had a live auction next for the larger items that were donated to us, for which a family friend was the auctioneer, and he did amazing.

Jen planned a dessert dash that went off spectacularly with almost all donated pies, cakes, and cookies. The night had come to an end, and it was almost a blur to me. So much work had gone into that day, and it felt unbelievable that I was part of making that happen.

We finally had gotten the place cleaned up, and all our stuff hauled out in trucks and trailers.

It was time to go home and really reflect on this day.

When I arrived home, my family was up visiting around the patio fire. Friends came over, and we had some beers. We just talked about the success of it all. I was exhausted.

What it all came down to was that on April 18, 2014, one day prior to what would have been Rowyn's second birthday, Raise for Rowyn raised over sixty thousand dollars in her honor.

I think it was safe to say that day was another act of God.

The first thing we planned to do was contact that Marysville family.

# Chapter Twenty Eight

BRYNN

## A GIFT SENT FROM HEAVEN

*"Every good and perfect gift comes from above."*
James 1:17

With my delivery of our new baby soon approaching, I knew I had some decisions to make regarding work.

Cody and I had discussed me staying home with the baby throughout my pregnancy, but he was not fully supportive of the idea right off the bat.

I spent many nights praying and asking God where He wanted me to be. I felt in my heart that I wanted nothing more than to be home for a while and soak up every single moment with my newborn as possible, while also spending more time growing our charity.

After many months of praying about it and asking for guidance, my answer was clear. I knew God wanted my focus on the charity and my home life.

As much as I tried to slow down my hectic schedule, it seemed impossible. God would keep placing these amazing opportunities in front of me for charity growth.

There was no denying that He wanted my focus there. I started preparing my clients and my salon family for the fact that I would not be returning to work after the baby was born.

It was emotional and foreign to me to even think of the idea of not planning on returning to the salon. I had been with the salon through both of my previous pregnancies and went back to work quickly after delivery. I have always prided myself on being independent and not wanting to rely on my husband financially, and I also loved my job.

It was never a question before of if I wanted to return to work, I just knew I did. Cody reluctantly started accepting the idea more and more of me staying home with the kids. It made him nervous to think he would have the bills to take care of all on his income, but I knew we could make it work, and I was fine cutting back on some things.

I had faith that God would provide for our family. This was something that caused some tension between us, but in my heart I just felt like I needed to be home.

We just had lost Rowyn and I was back at work three months later. I needed this time to cherish our new child as well as still grieve my loss.

The last year has been a blur, and I still have days that it doesn't seem real.

During one of our heated conversations, I was reassuring Cody that God will take care of us because this is where He wants me to be. He shouted, "God doesn't pay our bills, Brynn!"

I had to laugh out loud because he did have a valid point. Even though he was so reluctant and scared at the idea of living off his income alone, I was not scared about it at all. I just knew God had a different path for me, and my faith reassured me to follow his path.

The day I went into labor, I worked at the salon. I had gotten in all of my loyal clients and said my farewells to them, as I knew I wasn't returning.

I wasn't planning on that being my last day of work since it was still over two weeks until my due date, but I had an overwhelming sense that it very well may be.

When I was cleaning up for the evening, I shared with my coworkers, "This may be my last day here."

I felt prepared for the baby to come, and I knew she would arriving early. I was finally at ease with her arriving anytime.

That evening, I was exhausted. I really wanted to just stay home, prop up my cankles and watch a marathon of "The Real Housewives", but it was a new ladies night starting at our church and I really didn't want to miss it.

I stiffly peeled myself off the couch and made the two-minute drive down the road to church. Once I sat down there and began chatting with the ladies, I started to feel my contractions getting stronger.

I started watching the clock for the next hour, and they were moving closer together and progressing.

*This may be the real thing.*

Even though this was my third pregnancy, it was still hard to decipher if these were real contractions or just Braxton-Hicks.

The ladies said a prayer for me and the baby that evening before I left. I had to get back home quickly so Cody could go to work.

His terrible graveyard schedule was something I was used to, but it never seemed to get easier to deal with. I was home just before Wyatt's bedtime as Cody was racing out the door for work.

"This may be the night," I said.

"Really? Well, I'll keep my phone nearby. Keep me posted," he excitedly replied.

He was out the door and I started preparing Wyatt for bed.

Wyatt insisted he sleep with me, which had become our routine when Daddy worked nights. I cherished that snuggle time and loved giggling together over stories.

I wasn't feeling good but after he continued insisting, I let Wyatt climb into bed with me. My contractions were continuing to progress, and I was getting them five minutes apart for over an hour. I had been texting Cody the updates so he could prepare work if he had to leave. My pain was increasing, and I texted Cody: **Come HOME.**

He was about 40 minutes out, and I had a feeling she would come fast. Our hospital bags were packed and we were ready to go.

Cody called Sheri, his stepmother, on his way home, and she came over to stay with Wyatt for us. I still did not know if my contractions would keep up but knew I should be evaluated if this in fact was the real thing.

We arrived at the hospital around 2:30 A.M., and after being evaluated they concluded this was it. She would be arriving soon.

I had waited so long to meet her. I couldn't wait to hold another precious baby.

*What's she going to look like? Will she be a brunette like her dad? Will she look like Rowyn?*

My mind raced as I lay in the hospital bed.

I placed a photo of Rowyn across the room so I could focus on her. I wanted her there and I felt like she was. The thought of her being in the room with us brought me comfort, a sense of safety. I knew she would watch over us and her new baby sister.

Cody and I said a prayer. "Lord, please bless me with a safe delivery and a healthy baby. Please watch over us. Allow us, Lord, to feel Rowyn's presence in the room with us. Amen."

AT 10:35 A.M., ON October 16, 2015, Mynrow Leea Johnson made her grand arrival into the world.

The first glimpse I got of her, I knew something wasn't right.

Her color was dark, too dark.

It wasn't normal. She wouldn't let out a cry. Fear and anxiety paralyzed me. I immediately went back to that terrible place of thinking something was going to happen to her.

*I am going to lose another child.*

The medical team filled the room. They quickly had Mynrow over in the crib across the room from me. I could not see what was going on, but what I could see was concern on Cody's and my mom's faces. I knew the look.

Cody looked over at me and I could see the fear in his eyes, too. Every sense of comfort I had before left me completely. Tears started rolling down my cheeks. I looked over at Rowyn's picture and quietly stared, as I was talking to her in my head.

*Sissy, please take care of your baby sister. Watch over her. Please, don't let anything happen to her.*

They took Mynrow out of the room, into the intensive care nursery. I was preparing myself for bad news; instinctively, it was something that I did now.

You prepare yourself for another devastation. My doctor was reassuring me that everything was okay and not to worry. She was going to be just fine.

My blood pressure had dropped, and I was losing a lot of blood. I was stuck in my room for recovery and wasn't able to be with Mynrow.

The pediatrician came into my room shortly after and discussed what had happened with me. Mynrow had swallowed meconium and with her being on the early side, her lungs were not managing their oxygen levels on their own.

This entailed her being on oxygen support until she could breathe properly on her own. He reassured me as well that this was fairly common and not to worry, that she was going to be just fine.

Cody and my mom were in the nursery with Mynrow for what seemed like hours before they came back into my room.

My mom came in first. "She's absolutely beautiful," she said. "She has a full head of brown hair and looks just like Cody!"

"Really? Did you take a picture?" I asked.

I had not even been able to see what she looked like, so I was desperate to see her. My mom hadn't taken a picture, so my anticipation continued to grow.

Cody came into the room to check on me. "How are you doing?" he asked.

I stared at him, thinking to myself, *Well, that was a dumb question.* I didn't need to answer, as my expression gave it away. I could feel my eyes welling up with tears again, even though I was trying so hard to contain them.

"How is Mynrow? I just want to see her. Did you take any pictures?" I asked.

He pulled his phone from his pocket and handed it to me. Excitedly, I pulled up the few photos he had taken. She was hooked up to monitors and tiny breathing tubes; it was shocking to see her naked little body only in a diaper taken over by all these devices.

"You should get to go see her anytime," the nurse said.

What felt like an eternity, but was about five hours later, I was finally released out of recovery and able to go see Mynrow. The nurse wheeled me in a wheelchair over to her crib.

My first glimpse of her revealed her dark olive complexion and a head of dark brown hair like her daddy's. She looked so tiny.

I wanted to scoop her right out of the bassinet and swaddle her up.

My heart was instantly bursting with love, the kind that takes over every part of you. Completely overwhelmed again with emotions, I started to cry, unable to contain them that time.

I hadn't felt this much love in my heart for over a year, ever since Rowyn passed.

I knew God had sent this baby into our lives to give us hope and love. To give me something to keep fighting for.

The nurse carefully placed Mynrow in my arms. I couldn't believe the perfect little miracle I was holding.

She was a perfect gift from God.

I was mesmerized by her dark hair and skin; she was so opposite of the other kids. I was thrilled Cody finally got a baby who looked like him. I couldn't hold her long because she needed to go back under her warm light in the crib, but I cherished every minute I got to embrace her.

Cody and I sat with her for a long time and held her little hands.

She was a healthy seven pounds, eight ounces, and twenty-one inches long.

*Sissy, thank you for being such a good big sister and watching over Mynrow. Thank you for helping God pick out the perfect little baby for our family. I love you, baby girl.*

I knew Rowyn was there. Without a doubt, I knew she was watching over us and doing her best to keep her baby sister safe. I felt comfort knowing we had our own personal angel with us at all times.

# Chapter Twenty Nine

## CASSIE

### A TESTING YEAR

*"What Grief does is it puts us squarely in the middle of a fire, and it burns away everything that is not essential to our lives."*
*Alana Sheeran*

Reaching out to the Marysville family was something that became a very important milestone in our story.

It was a family that had endured a very similar heartache as we had, at such a unique time, the day of our big event.

Brynn had told me once, "I feel like the families we are supposed to help will be brought forth by God."

In other words, it would be obvious.

It seems like these tragedies are all around us, but we never noticed it as much before.

Just as we began to seek out families, they began to seek out us.

We were finding ourselves busier and busier, even though we had added the additional team members.

From my perception, I wake up and get the kids around and out the door to daycare so I can go to work.

After my five-hour shift, I pick them up, run any errands I need to run and head home to start dinner and work on chores.

In between all of this work at home, I am checking and responding to emails. Calling funeral homes, families, and working on upcoming events.

The work with Raise for Rowyn has never stopped, or even slowed down for that matter. I think we all thought that would maybe happen at one point, but it definitely has not.

This has been one of the biggest struggles with my family life and my marriage.

My husband is proud and supportive of the charity, but it does take a lot of the time that we have together away. It has been an adjustment for him to see me on a phone or an iPad even more than I was before.

This has become a gigantic part of my life, occupying a large part of my time. It has been an adjustment for our family.

If you remember from the beginning, Tenino is not my hometown. I first moved here with just a couple of friends and spent a lot of time alone with our yellow lab puppy, Sunny.

I had nothing to occupy my time besides Aaron and my dog. I was that strange twenty-four-year-old girl in Petco, on a Saturday night during hunting season, walking my puppy around. I say hunting season, because these were the only times I was not with my best friend, Aaron.

As time progressed and we have built our own life and family, I have also built my own friendships.

I now have a group of women here who love and support me so much we are like a little family. I knew I had these good friends, but this last year I really learned just how good these friends are.

No discredit to my wonderful husband, but the words, advice, and even laughter you can get from a platonic relationship with your girlfriends is so healthy and needed in dark times.

Days when I could not stand myself, who I was, what I had done, and the overwhelming feeling of guilt, it was them who could make me feel better. Or at least human.

Wanting to be around the girls more often has not always been easy for Aaron to understand, either.

Just as my life was in survival mode, his was changing also as he watched his wife and our life together do a one-eighty.

Between our new charity, the church and my friendships, we have found ourselves spending even less time together. To top it all off, taking the demotion at work and dropping to part-time has made an even bigger dent in our life and lifestyle.

Money was not something we had to worry too much about before. Not realizing it at the time, God had taken care of us. Now, we are still trying to find a budget that will work for us, as we are not as able to do things like we used to.

It has been undoubtedly a difficult year, and we are still learning to navigate the new life while grieving our old one. Ultimately, I wish I could give my husband the dreams and goals I had before, which was making more money and building our dream home on acreage. They are still there, but they are not what are important to me in the now.

As the Raise for Rowyn work was picking up, we ordered new merchandise and continued receiving support from our followers.

We held a rummage sale in our church parking lot, raising over five thousand dollars.

We built a float and rode through Tenino during 'Oregon Trail Days' to say thank you to our community.

The float ended up taking first place in the parade.

We were the beneficiaries of the Olympia Pub Crawl, which was a tremendous opportunity for us to get out in the Olympia area. Amazingly, before the event even took place, they made us the beneficiaries for 2016.

We held a 3D archery competition, and despite the pouring rain and the wind, we came out successfully ahead. Everything that Rowyn's name has been a part of has been a complete success.

When August came around this year, just one month prior to the one-year anniversary of our accident, I hit one of my biggest falls in depression.

I had not been in that place for months, and it felt impossible that I would get out from it. I knew I could, though, because I had done it before.

I literally found myself unable to function. I would get my kids to daycare then return home to my bed.

I remember lying there once and looking down the hall across the house into the bathroom, at the bathtub. I wanted to take a bath so badly. I kept thinking about all of the reasons I wanted to do it.

Something as a mom we never get enough alone time to do.

But I couldn't get up. I mentally wanted to, but I also mentally could not. This is something that, prior to my own difficulties with this diagnosis, I had no clue how people could feel that way. I read medical records for a living, and constantly see people struggling with depression and anxiety.

Never could I have ever really understood or even empathized with that feeling, until now.

I know how it feels to forget to brush your teeth and even shower.

I have gone out in public looking ways I never thought in a million years I would allow myself to do. I just did not care.

It was during this time in early August that I had to pick up a banner at Brynn's house for a friend to use in a parade in Morton, Washington.

They offered to put the Raise for Rowyn banner on the truck they were driving through town that day.

I drove to her house, as I had many times before. I got out and noticed the grass was turning brown, like it was that day back in September.

Things were beginning to look eerily similar to that day almost a year before.

As I walked in her door, she greeted me with a hug, saying, "How are you doing today?"

I didn't even have to say anything because the tears just started coming out of nowhere.

She hugged me tighter and said, "I'm so sorry you are having such a hard time. I could have brought this to you."

It was just another moment in time where I received comfort from what some might think of as the most unlikely source. She can relate to those days like nobody else ever fully can.

During this difficult time, I ended up taking two to three weeks off work again. I left town on a whim with my kids and went to the Tri-Cities to be around my family.

I needed to feel something, *anything*.

It helped, but the feelings did not subside there. Brynn had taken on my Raise for Rowyn duties for the month and the rest of the team picked up slack as we were approaching the archery competition.

It was at that time I was reached out to by a journalist in Los Angeles named Georgie.

She had actually contacted us several months prior, but a journalist from Florida was doing a story on us for a magazine in the United Kingdom.

By that time, we were no longer in a contract with the journalist from Florida, and Georgie had expressed that she had never stopped thinking about our story.

She asked about interest in being featured in anything in the United States, which of course we were because it's publicity for our charity. After telling her our story, that was about all.

She wanted to wait to release the story in the *Daily Mail* until our anniversary date, hoping that would pique some interest.

Essentially, we were waiting, but not expecting anything to really come out of it, so it was really easy to just forget about it.

I returned to work at one point, and despite my anxiety, I was determined I was going to make it.

That day, we had a mandatory staff meeting where unexpectedly, I was called up to the front of the room. I just couldn't do that kind of stuff anymore, especially at that very fragile time where I was trying to recoup.

I began to cry during my walk to the front, and ended up leaving shortly after in a downpour of emotion.

I was embarrassed.

*Who is this person?*

*How can I not keep it together anymore for anything?*

I quickly packed up my things and left the office, crying the whole way home. As I climbed in my bed, I prayed to the Lord to please let me wake up feeling better.

*I do not want to feel this depression anymore.*

To my surprise, I did wake up feeling a little better.

In the days following, I regained myself a little bit more and more.

Then it came, the dreaded September. I told Brynn, "I will be the strong one this month like you were last month."

Somehow, since Raise for Rowyn started, our ups and downs have tended to fall opposite of one another.

Oddly enough, as emotionally and mentally draining as September was, it was not my worst month of the last year.

It was the night before the anniversary, and my husband had been out of town on his annual elk hunting trip.

I had my in-laws taking my children overnight so I could feel what I needed to feel and lose it if I needed to. I didn't want to have to keep it together for anyone.

I was surprised to learn that my girlfriends had all arranged to come over to be with me that evening so I was not alone. It was another amazing expression of the valuable friendships I have needed this past year.

I had been in a therapy appointment earlier in the day. When I got out, I noticed I had a message on my personal Facebook from a name I did not recognize.

Since starting the charity, this was not surprising because I had gotten them many times before. I really just did not have it in me to open the message, so I put it off. I had been in touch with Brynn briefly that day, but I knew she was really struggling.

It was about 4:00 on that Tuesday night when I decided to open the message. It was from an associate producer of the *Dr. Phil* show who wanted to discuss our story.

I immediately was shocked, and anxious about the message. I contacted Georgie, and to her surprise the story was released the day prior to our anniversary.

It was within an hour that the preliminary plans of flying to L.A. that upcoming Sunday were in the works.

I texted Brynn, letting her know I realized she was having a terrible time, but we had just been contacted by the *Dr. Phil* show. She was as shocked as I was, of course, but was in no condition to deal with the plans so she asked me to do it.

It was about twenty minutes later when Brynn actually called me. She was sitting at her house in mid-prayer with God and Rowyn, asking for direction as to whether or not this was something we should pursue, when her home telephone rang.

A phone number only a handful of people even have.

It was *Inside Edition*, wanting to know about having us on the show.

There we were in what should have been the hardest, most emotional evening of the year for us, and we were in talks of taking our charity on national television. God was working for us that day, helping to coat our pain with excitement and another reminder of the positive this tragic accident had brought forth.

Brynn ended up coming over to be surrounded with women to share in the good company. She was carrying Rowyn's stuffed pink bunny around.

It was beautiful and sad at the same time.

I imagine she was reliving the last day, night and morning she had with Rowyn a year before. I know my mind went back to that place. I also imagined she was thinking it had been 365 days since she had touched, smelled, heard her laughter, seen her face, and held her baby girl in her arms.

My pregnant friend, resting a stuffed bunny on her belly as she sat on my couch a year after I had accidentally run over her daughter and took her life.

Yes, God absolutely had our backs.

That Sunday morning, Brynn was dropped off at my house early and we left for the Portland airport. I had just spent the last four days in Victoria B.C. with my mom on a getaway she planned for us during this dreaded anniversary. It was a very special trip we had, and now we were on to L.A.

When we arrived at LAX, we saw a man near baggage claim in a black suit, dark sunglasses, a luggage cart and a sign that said 'Mrs. Johnson'.

I nudged Brynn and said, "Do you think that's for us?"

I can't remember if he said it first or if it was Brynn, but somehow we made the *Dr. Phil* show connection, and he loaded our bags and we followed him to a fancy black Escalade.

As we drove to the *Dr. Phil* loft, he narrated where we were and what we were seeing. We were told prior that at the loft, we would do about an hour of filming for the show that day and to come camera-ready.

We were unsure of what to expect, but it was exciting for both of us. They brought us to a room that looked like a living room in a house. This loft consisted of multiple rooms on two floors, all portraying a different room in a house. One was a bedroom, there was a kitchen, and several rooms with couches.

There were two cameramen and a woman who did all of the questioning. They pulled Brynn into a room first and filmed her telling the story of that dreadful day. I could hear her talking through her tears, and it was difficult. In the meantime, we were told they wanted to film us on our website.

Our website had been getting a complete facelift, so I quickly reached out to our board member Jen who was working on this project. It was very nerve-racking because we didn't want to pull up the website and have it not work.

I should have known God had us through that one, as well. I got a text from Jen saying it would be live within fifteen minutes.

For her and our close friend Megan to pull this off in such a short amount of time was likely impossible, but not for God.

When it was my turn to tell my story, it was also very difficult and emotional.

By the time I finished, we had been at the loft already for about three hours.

Then they filmed us sitting on some of the furniture in the different rooms, and pulling up our website. We were walking around outside, staring off into the distance, just feeling like a couple of goobers to be quite honest.

When we were finally done at the loft, we were taken to our hotel, the Sheraton Universal. It was gorgeous, and we had a beautiful view of the Hollywood hills.

We finally ate dinner at around 8:00, which for a pregnant woman is way too late. We had all day Monday to do whatever we wanted to do. We took the little shuttle up to Universal City, rode a really dirty subway to Hollywood Boulevard, had non-alcoholic drinks by the pool and worked consistently all day with Louisa at LM Creations in Australia, who was finalizing our book cover.

We were not scheduled for the cover to be done until mid-October, but because we hoped to get it on the air for *Dr. Phil*, Louisa worked some serious magic for us.

ON TUESDAY MORNING, WE were picked up and taken to the *Dr. Phil* show for filming at 8:30.

We were brought to our dressing room, taken for hair and makeup, and then dressed by the wardrobe department.

As we were called into the hallway, we had someone attaching microphones to our shirts, someone dusting us with lint rollers and touch-ups by the hair and makeup crew. We were directed downstairs, where we sat in a room with rows of chairs and a TV.

All the while, we were hoping to get to meet Oprah. We hadn't even met Phil yet. Unfortunately, she left as soon as her portion on the show was done and we did not get to meet her.

However, after seeing how all of this showbiz stuff really goes down, I am not that disappointed.

In a matter of minutes, Brynn and I were on deck, saying a quick prayer together, and then walking out to the live studio audience.

I was not as nervous as I had thought I would be out there, and in fact quite calm, actually. We were a little disappointed that a lot of our interviews were cut out, especially the message about our faith in our process of healing, as well as more of the positives of Raise for Rowyn.

However, it went how it was supposed to go, when it was supposed to go, and for as long as it was supposed to go, because God had it arranged already.

We were blessed with the opportunity to share the deepest part of our hearts with the millions of viewers of the *Dr. Phil* show.

A LITTLE OVER A WEEK after the show, October 15th, Mynrow Leea Johnson was brought into this world and held a far greater meaning than anyone could ever realize.

Mynrow was born one year, one month, and one day from the day Rowyn passed away. Brynn once told me the number for angels was 111. Could it be Mynrow was our little angel?

As the pictures began to come in through text and our Raise for Rowyn messenger, I could not have been more excited to see what Mynrow looked like.

I had been at the hospital earlier in the day, just after Brynn had her, but I had not yet gotten to see her. It was such an overwhelming day of emotion, and it hit me so unexpectedly. I knew the day Mynrow arrived would be so beautiful, but I did not anticipate all of the other emotions that came with it.

I cried a lot that day, more than I had in a while.

As I sat in my living room with my girlfriends and watched the *Dr. Phil* show air, I continued to shed tears. I had a couple of beers and tried to just let the feelings come over me instead of try to dissect them.

I was messaging with Brynn. She was in a hospital room with the women in her family watching, while little Mynrow remained in the NICU.

Knowing Mynrow had been in the NICU for a little while, I did not want to throw myself into the family's intimate time as they welcomed their precious new baby. I ended up going to see Mynrow for the first time on Saturday morning, October 17th. Mynrow was two days old.

WHEN I WALKED IN the house, Brynn and her mom, Janet had just placed her headband back on to turn her to my view.

It was like that 'love at first sight' feeling you don't get with everyone's babies.

You get that feeling with your own children, of course, and your nieces and nephews, but the feeling that came over me when I held Mynrow was much the same. She is such an important piece to this whole story, and she certainly feels like a piece of Rowyn and a symbol of Heaven.

For her to arrive on the day we shared the story on national news was so perfect. It was as if her little soul was thinking, *This is going to be a hard day for my family, so I'm going to spice it up a little.*

As I stared at her tiny features, her calmness and warmth filled up my heart.

In fact, she was so calm I got scared a couple of times that she wasn't breathing.

Everything about her says she is her daddy's girl, especially her beautiful skin tone.

Right off the bat, though, I noticed she had Rowyn's chin. The chin I loved to squeeze every time I saw her, the one I had squeezed on the day of our accident for the last time.

I immediately reached down and gave it a gentle squeeze.

I watched Cody leave for an evening hunt that day, holding his baby girl before he left.

I watched him look happy as he spoke to her and of her. I watched him kiss Brynn and tell her he loved her before he left the house.

It was an intimacy between them I had not seen before, and a love between them you could almost feel.

"It seems like you guys are doing so great. You seem so happy," I said to Brynn.

"You know," she replied, "we talked on the way home from the hospital, and as much as we wish we could have Rowyn right here with us on Earth, we are at peace knowing our family has the best guardian angel out there. We know she is with us all the time."

It almost brought me to tears.

As I sat in her living room, with Mynrow back in my arms, I felt a sense of peace come over me, too.

To see this family so brokenhearted for a whole year, and to know I was involved in their devastation has been unbearable at times.

Now, I see this family rebuilding what Satan tried to destroy, which is their family, happiness and faith. It is a true testimony of the Lord.

In some way, even though we have been doing it all along for the last year, it feels okay to move forward. It feels like the right thing to look forward, even if we still look back a lot.

The visions of that September day will likely never fully leave me, and just this morning on my drive to work I saw that blood-stained robe flash before my eyes.

However, even though I see those things, I can choose to see the path ahead and feel okay about it.

# Chapter Thirty

### BRYNN|

## A HEALING HEART

*This is what the LORD says: I have heard your prayer and
seen your tears. I will heal you.*
*2 Kings 20:5*

It has now been two weeks since Mynrow's birth.

We have started another new chapter in our lives.

I never expected to feel so much love in my heart again, especially only a year after Rowyn passed, but I do. It's truly a miracle.

After losing my child, I never thought I would be able to experience happiness ever again, let alone feel joy.

I feel like I have purpose again.

I love being a mother to a new baby, and I am soaking up every little moment I can.

I am calmer now, able to enjoy it more because I know how precious this time is.

I know this child was sent to our family to help mend our broken hearts, and it has helped.

My love for Rowyn will never fade or be replaced by Mynrow, but I know Rowyn had so much to do with sending us the gift of another healthy little girl.

I still have hard days, and find myself still searching the room looking for Rowyn, but I am slowly accepting her new role in our lives.

Her soul is still here.

She is with us, still shining her light and touching lives all over the world.

I look at the impact that my tiny seventeen-month-old daughter has had on so many people, and it is astonishing.

She had such a short time here on Earth, but she has changed people's lives.

She has inspired me to be a better person, a better mother, and grow my faith in God.

I know she's always watching me and wanting me to succeed and overcome this pain.

I go on for her in a way. It would have been so easy to give up and not care about anything, but she has kept me going to where I am today.

Healing gracefully, enjoying my time with family, cherishing those moments just a little bit more with my children, running a rapidly growing non-profit, and continuing to grow my relationship with God and Rowyn on the other side.

I have a new feeling of contentment with my new life. It will always be a hard pill to swallow, though; I will still never want to accept that I lost my child.

It will always be hard, and I wouldn't want it to be easy, but for where I am now in my life, I can say I am happy again.

I hope sharing my story of pain, grief, faith, and love can inspire someone to keep fighting the battle.

Have hope that you can overcome your heartache and live happily again.

It takes time.

Losing a child is the hardest battle to face, but don't give up.

Grow your faith and cling to whatever comfort and support you have.

Family, friends and faith will get you through.

If I didn't have those things, I wouldn't be where I am today.

God has brought me joy again in ways I never expected. I will continue for the rest of my days honoring my daughter Rowyn's life.

I am so blessed to be her mommy and spend the time that we did get together. I want to make her proud.

My goal is to continue to grow our charity in her name and help inspire more families all over the country.

My family and I will continue to always honor the life of an angel.

GOD CAN *restore* WHAT IS *broken* AND CHANGE
IT INTO *something* AMAZING.
ALL YOU NEED IS *faith* .
JOEL 2:25

# Acknowledgments
## BRYNN JOHNSON

I would like to thank God for inspiring me to write this book.

My angel daughter Rowyn for motivating me to keep going when I didn't think I had anything left.

Shey Stahl for leading me in the right directions to accomplish my goals.

Cassie and her family for their commitment to our book, charity, and healing together.

My family and friends for always supporting me and surrounding me with love.

My pastor and his wife, Jim and Stacey Ford, for filling my heart with hope and faith.

My Raise for Rowyn team for keeping our charity growing strong.

Without the love and support from so many, I would never have been able to accomplish my dream of writing this book.

# Acknowledgments
## CASSIE MILLER

First and foremost, thank you to God for getting me through the most unbearable time of my life, while continuing to be a place of refuge for me.

To Shey Stahl for encouraging us to write and helping us through the entire process of becoming authors and publishing our story.

To my husband Aaron, supporting me throughout this last year, as you have had to deal with my emotional instability as well as watch me glued to my iPad much of the time.

To Brynn, Cody and your families. Thank you for allowing me to tell this story from my perspective, and continuing to stand by my family and I despite how difficult this has been for everyone.

To our parents Debbie, Keith, Lisa, Dan, brother Cody and sister-in-law Kelli. Thank you for being such a supportive family and giving me strength, encouragement and refuge when I needed it most.

To my Grandma Neaty, whom I was able to spend her last month in this life with, due to this horrific accident. You are with me always, and I am comforted knowing Rowyn has an extra grandma in Heaven, you.

To my girlfriends, all of you. Hometown friends, Tenino friends, college friends, and work friends. Without you, I do not know if I could be standing tall today.

To the Raise for Rowyn board members, for carrying extra weight at times and sharing the passion for the cause.

To Pastor Jim & New Day Christian Center. Thank you for welcoming our families at the most broken time in our lives. I am grateful to consider New Day my church, and you all my church family.

# Meet Author
## BRYNN JOHNSON

Brynn Johnson began writing shortly after losing her seventeen-month-old daughter Rowyn due to a tragic accident.

Through writing, she has found a sense of healing, sharing her personal struggles as well as her testimony of faith. She has spent her last year growing a non-profit organization, Raise for Rowyn, in honor of her daughter.

Raise for Rowyn provides financial and emotional assistance to other families who are also struggling with the loss of a child.

Brynn and her husband Cody are parents to three beautiful children, recently welcoming another baby girl into their family. They reside in Tenino, Washington, a rural, close-knit community. Brynn's passionate about being a mother and wife and enjoys spending her free time with family, cooking, hiking, camping, and crafting.

In previous years, she spent her time as a hair stylist and just recently became a stay-at-home momma. She feels fulfillment helping others through her charity and sharing her journey of grief to offer hope to others.

You can keep in touch with Brynn on Facebook at:
https://www.facebook.com/authorbrynnjohnson/?fref=t s

# Meet Author
## CASSIE MILLER

Cassie Miller was raised in the small town of Benton City, Washington, by her two loving parents, Keith and Debbie, and older brother, Cody.

She attended college at Central Washington University, where in 2005 she received her BA in public relations. By 2007, she made her way to western Washington, where she now resides with Aaron, her husband of four-and-a-half years, and their two sons, Easton and Logan.

After her involvement in the horrific accident with Rowyn Leea Johnson, she dropped to a part-time position with the State of Washington, so she is able to spend more time being a mother and enjoying the simpler things in life.

In addition, she is the co-founder and vice president of the non-profit organization, Raise for Rowyn.

Raise for Rowyn assists families with funeral/mortuary expenses, and also provides emotional support to those struggling with the loss of a child. In between work and raising a family, Cassie coaches her son's soccer team and helps in the nursery at her church.

You can keep in touch with Cassie on Facebook at:

https://www.facebook.com/authorcassiemiller/?fref=ts

IN HONOR OF ANGEL ROWYN

The mission of the Raise for Rowyn foundation is to provide financial assistance to families within our surrounding communities who are struggling with the loss of a child.

In April of 2015, Raise for Rowyn accepted their first dime in a venture to do something neither of us had ever done before.

We had a mission to help families with funeral and mortuary expenses. With Rowyn in the front of our minds, and a path lead only by God himself, we have easily surpassed meeting the goal, had there been one.

By October 2015, in just a six-month period, Raise for Rowyn has successfully helped twenty-six grieving families. This small Tenino, Washington charity, which does not even have an office, has paid out $36,922.47 to funeral homes.

In this journey, we are blessed to have supportive team members, husbands, families, friends, our church, and all of the followers who have watched, prayed, and shared our story. We will be continuing to help families in these situations, being an ear to listen for others when they are lost in devastation, and grow as people while growing the charity.

We know Rowyn is proud of us, and we will do whatever it takes to continue to make her proud during this lifetime.

If you would like to donate to Raise for Rowyn or would like more information about our foundation, please visit:

http://www.raiseforrowyn.org/

You can also contact us on Facebook at: https://www.facebook.com/Raise-for-Rowyn-1525825754354063/?fref=ts

Twitter: https://twitter.com/RaiseForRowyn

Instagram: https://instagram.com/raise4rowyn/

*Team members of Raise for Rowny at the 5k Run in April 2015*

Cassie and Brynn at the Burger Claim

*Board members of Raise for Rowyn at the Oly Pub Crawl*

*Easton Miller and Wyatt Johnson supporting Raise for Rowyn*

# PERSONAL *photographs* FROM *The* JOHNSON FAMILY

*Brynn and Cody Johnson*

*Brynn and Cody on their wedding day ~ March 19, 2010*

*Brynn and Wyatt ~ 6 months old*

*Rowyn Leea Johnson*

*Wyatt Randall Johnson ~ Age 3*

*Rowyn looking cute ~ 7 months old*

*Rowyn, her big brother Wyatt and their daddy, Cody*
*September 2014*

*Rowyn and her mommy and daddy*
*September 6, 2014*

*Wyatt at Rowyn's grave*
*Easter 2015*

*The Johnson Family in Hawaii*

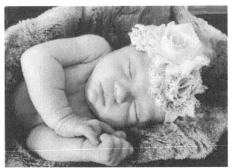

*Mynrow Leea Johnson*
*Rowyn's baby sister*

*Cassie and Brynn with baby Mynrow*
*October 2015*

# PERSONAL *photographs* FROM *the* MILLER FAMILY

*Cassie and her husband Aaron ~ June 17, 2012*

*Aaron and Cassie*

*Aaron, Cassie and Easton*

*The Miller Family*

*Best Friends Easton and Wyatt ~ Spring 2015*

*Easton age 4 and Logan age 1*

*Logan*

*Easton*

*Cassie and her boys*

*Cassie and Brynn at a Raise for Rowyn event*

*Cassie holding baby Mynrow*

47557660R00168

Made in the USA
Middletown, DE
08 June 2019